Housing Redux

The Edward P. Bass
Distinguished Visiting Architecture Fellowship

HOUSING

Yale School of Architecture

REDUX

Nnenna Lynch
Edward P. Bass Distinguished Visiting Architecture Fellow

with
James von Klemperer
Hana Kassem
Andrei Harwell

edited by
Nina Rappaport
Saba Salekfard

Yale School of Architecture
180 York Street
New Haven, CT 06520
www.architecture.yale.edu

Distributed by Actar
355 Lexington Avenue, 8th floor
New York, NY 10017
www.actar.com

Housing Redux was made possible through an endowment from the Edward P. Bass
Distinguished Visiting Architecture Fellowship at the Yale School of Architecture.
It is the 17th in a series of publications produced through the dean's office.

Editors: Nina Rappaport and Saba Salekfard
Text Editor: Cathryn Drake
Design: Manuel Miranda Practice
Library of Congress data available upon request.
ISBN: 978-1-63840-081-3

Table of Contents

Edward P. Bass Distinguished Visiting Architecture Fellowship

In 2003 Edward P. Bass (Yale College '67), who graduated from the Yale School of Architecture in 1972, endowed this fellowship for property developers to lead advanced studios in collaboration with design faculty. An environmentalist, Bass sponsored the Biosphere 2 development in Oracle, Arizona, in 1991. As a developer he is contributing to the ongoing revitalization of downtown Fort Worth, Texas, where his project Sundance Square, combining restoration and new construction, has transformed a moribund urban core into a vibrant regional center. In his work Bass has been guided by the conviction that architecture is a socially engaged art operating at the intersection of grand visions and everyday realities.

The Bass Fellowship ensures that the school curriculum recognizes the role of property developers as integral to the design process by inviting them to work with educators and architecture students in the studio and contextualize the practice of architecture within the wider professional discourse. The following are the former Bass Fellowship studios:

2005
Poetry, Property, and Place
Gerald Hines and Stefan Behnisch

2006
Future Proofing
Stuart Lipton, Richard Rogers, Chris Wise, and Malcolm Smith

Spring 2007
The Human City: Kings Cross
Roger Madelin and Demetri Porphyrios

Fall 2007
Urban Integration:
Bishopsgate Goods Yard
Nick Johnson and FAT Architects

2008
Learning in Las Vegas
Chuck Atwood and David M. Schwarz

2010
Urban Intersections: São Paulo
Katherine Farley and Deborah Berke

2011
Rethinking Chongqing:
Mixed Use and Super Dense
Vincent Lo, Paul Katz, James von Klemperer, and Forth Bagley

2012
Social Infrastructure:
New York
Douglas Durst and Bjarke Ingles

2013
The Marine Etablissement:
New Terrain for
Central Amsterdam
Isaäc Kalisvaart, Alexander Garvin,
Kevin D. Gray, and Andrei Harwell

2013
A Sustainable Bodega/
Hotel in Rioja
John Spence, Andy Bow,
Patrick Bellew, and Timothy Newton

2015
Paranoazinho:
City-Making Beyond Brasilia
Rafael Birmann and Sunil Bald

2015
Harlem: Mart 125
Jonathan Rose, Sara Caples,
and Everardo Jefferson

2016
Mixed-Use Regeneration
Jonathan Emery, James von
Klemperer, and Forth Bagley

2017
The Diamonds of American Cities
Janet Marie Smith, Alan Plattus,
and Andrei Harwell

2018
...And More
Michael Samuelian, Simon
Hartmann, and Andrei Harwell

2019
Next Generation Tourism:
Touching the Ground Lightly
John Spence, Henry Squire,
Patrick Bellew, and Timothy Newton

2020
The Innovative Urban Workplace
Abby Hamlin, Dana Tang, and
Andrei Harwell

INTRODUCTION

Nina Rappaport
Saba Salekfard

Housing Redux presents the design projects created by students for the 17th Edward P. Bass Distinguished Visiting Architecture Fellowship in a studio at the Yale School of Architecture. This edition was led by Nnenna Lynch, Bass Fellow and founder of Xylem Projects; James von Klemperer and Hana Kassem, principals at Kohn Pedersen Fox; and Andrei Harwell, faculty member at the Yale School of Architecture.

The studio investigated the New York City Housing Authority (NYCHA) typology and Washington Houses, in East Harlem, with the intent of proposing new architectural solutions "addressing the city's affordable-housing shortage while tackling questions of urban fabric and context, public and private space, and mixed-use development as a tool for connectivity." The students researched the history and current state of New York public housing to inform new models for inclusive and equitable development as alternatives to the status quo. Projects focused on urban design, ground-plane development, existing building alterations, and new building design as proposed interventions. The ultimate aim of the semester was to rethink the affordable-housing formula in new approaches while addressing equity challenges and incorporating mixed-use programming.

The first few weeks of the studio were dedicated to examining historical and contemporary housing typologies, both international and domestic, followed by student presentations of low- and mixed-income housing examples from their own hometowns. Following a site visit to Washington Houses, students formed teams to present a master plan framework, outlining key program elements, density goals, and strategies for wellness, sustainability, and resilience. For the remainder of the semester the students developed individual projects from their proposed master plans and explored possibilities for new buildings, renovations of existing buildings, and landscape alterations.

This book opens with the design brief outlining the studio's intent and challenges. It describes the historical context and current state of NYCHA projects and presents the studio project at the intersection of architecture, planning, and equity. The students reviewed current development proposals for other NYCHA properties and spoke with residents to inform their projects. The middle section of the book provides an introduction to the Washington Houses project, followed by a discussion on teaching and affordable housing organized by Nina Rappaport with visiting professors Hana Kassem, Nnenna Lynch, James von Klemperer, and Heather Roberge, the Davenport Visiting Professor.

The fifth and sixth sections of the book explore the students' research findings, master plan proposals, and project designs. Building on an analysis of the project site, requirements, and opportunities, students divided into teams to propose programs that add density to the master plan for three blocks. They then identified portions of the master plan to develop individually for the remainder of the semester. The project proposals explored a range of landscape and ground-plane additions, existing facade and interior renovations, and new buildings.

The editors would like to thank the students in the classes of 2022 and 2023 for their valuable contributions to the production of this book: Claudia Ansorena, Lindsay Duddy, Vignesh Harikrishnan, Suhyan Jang, Raul Martinez Martinez, Dominiq Oti, Saba Salekfard, David Scurry, and Levi Shaw-Faber. We would also like to extend our gratitude to text editor Cathryn Drake and the graphic designers at Manuel Miranda Practice.

Nnenna Lynch
James von Klemperer
Hana Kassem
Andrei Harwell

Introduction

The health of a society can be evaluated by the way it shelters the broadest cross section of its population. Large urban residential housing developments play a major role in determining the well-being of city dwellers, not only within but also surrounding them. The studio examined the importance of architecture in addressing equity through its most fundamental role—housing—focusing on the largest public-housing program in the United States, the New York City Housing Authority (NYCHA).

Recent events, such as the COVID-19 pandemic, heightened the importance of studying the intersection of planning, architecture, and equity. Related health-care challenges revealed how inequities in living conditions affect residents of low-income housing developments more severely than the larger population, due to density of habitation in flood-prone areas; overcrowding of apartments, facilitating viral spread; proximity to highways, leading to poor air quality and in turn high asthma rates; and lack of access to healthy food, promoting diabetes and obesity. Meanwhile New York City has an affordable-housing crisis, with two low-income households for every unit of affordable housing available.[1]

The studio familiarized students with the history and present state of New York City public housing and challenged them to propose improvements and alternatives to the status quo. Working in teams, the class focused on Washington Houses, on East 100th Street between Second and Third Avenues, to formulate programs promoting the rich culture of art, music, and social activism that generations of Spanish Harlem residents have created over the past 70 years as well as solutions to the health deficits and economic difficulties that stand in the way of societal well-being. The students analyzed examples of successful housing programs around the globe and learned about real-world business-development strategies to frame their design proposals in economic reality without compromising innovative thinking and design.

The New York Housing Authority (NYCHA) and Equitable Housing for New Yorkers

New York City maintains the largest public-housing stock of any city in the United States, accommodating roughly five percent of the city's three million households. Nineteenth-century housing conditions, particularly those for the working poor, were overcrowded, cheaply constructed, and unhealthy, as a result of rapid industrial growth and massive migration from Europe. Progressive urban reformers such as Catherine Bauer, Jacob Riis, Lewis Mumford, and others pressed for housing reforms to create safer, more sanitary accommodations for the growing population. During the Great

1 New York City Housing Plan, https://www1.nyc.gov/site/housing/problem/problem.page

Migration of African Americans from the U.S. South to the North, European immigrants arrived in New York in large numbers between 1910 and '40, with very few options for housing.

The earliest subsidized housing projects were developed with private funds provided by benefactors or foundations—for instance the Dunbar Apartments, in Harlem, built by John D. Rockefeller Jr. With the onset of the Great Depression in 1929, housing conditions in the city worsened as many residents found themselves without work. In parallel with Franklin Delano Roosevelt's new housing policies, such as the 1934 Housing Act, the New York City Housing Authority (NYCHA) was the first public-housing authority in the country, initiated to respond to the housing crisis. Designed by Frederick Ackerman, First Houses was the first public-housing project, constructed on the Lower East Side in 1935 on land donated by the Astor family. NYCHA continued by demolishing tenements through eminent domain and replacing them with new "modern" subsidized housing.

Heavily influenced by the principles of European Modernist housing including Le Corbusier's Ville Radieuse and Ludwig Hilberseimer's Zeilenbau, architects working for NYCHA, such as Swiss-born William Lescaze, designed projects as counterpoints to the congested, street-oriented low-rise buildings of the city. Frequently these were built as superblocks with freestanding slab or cruciform towers rotated away from the city grid and separated by substantial open space. The redbrick buildings were characteristically monofunctional and stylistically austere, with small window openings and few public amenities but ample open space. Community facilities were often integrated into the overall plans as one- or two-story buildings connected to the landscape. Following the Second World War, NYCHA housing development was accelerated and aided by a partnership with the lead planner for the city, Robert Moses. The majority of NYCHA developments were constructed between 1945 and '65 as part of a process that Moses hoped would reshape New York into a modern metropolis.

NYCHA's public-housing developments—325 across five boroughs—include single- and double-family houses and apartments, and shared small building units. Many of these facilities have community rooms and public facilities, but in some cases there are large income and racial disparities with the surrounding neighborhood or community.

Funding challenges for NYCHA since the late 1960s resulted first from a massive contraction of New York's economy (the city nearly became bankrupt in 1975) and then with changes in both housing policy and the politics of public housing at the municipal, state, and national levels. Starved for resources and aging rapidly, much of NYCHA's housing stock is in need of revitalization. Since the 1960s, continuing migration to New York from different parts of the world, especially from Latin and South America, coupled with skyrocketing real estate prices has brought more demand than ever for housing that is affordable, comfortable, convenient, healthy, and safe.

In an attempt to halt the rising deferred costs of upkeep for NYCHA and mitigate the unmet need for more affordable housing, mayor Bill de Blasio released a plan in 2015 called "Next Gen NYCHA" to address funding and maintenance concerns by "revamping management practices and generate revenue by building mixed-income and affordable housing on what the city deemed underused NYCHA land and by using new federal programs to shift NYCHA apartments over to Section 8, a more stable source of federal funding."[2] With highly constrained budgets, NYCHA is looking for new strategies that will allow it to upgrade and improve existing facilities while continuing to expand housing opportunities for New Yorkers.

One such program, established in 2022, leverages available land and unused FAR (Floor Area Ratio) while partnering with private developers to solve the housing shortage and deferred property maintenance. Under the Permanent Affordability Commitment Together (PACT), selected NYCHA properties are converted to Project-Based Section 8, which will open access to a reliable funding stream and in turn enable the properties to be properly maintained. A developer enters into a ground lease and takes on an extensive scope of work, including the repair and refurbishment of existing units and buildings, as well as the development of new housing and mixed-use facilities. The developer also serves as the new on-site property manager and partners with nonprofits to offer social services and community programs in new or repurposed community spaces. The PACT program formed the theoretical basis of our studio proposal.

Studio Proposal

This studio aimed to envision new architectural solutions for the NYCHA Washington Houses development to address the city's housing shortage as well as questions of urban fabric and context, public and private space, and mixed-use development as a tool for connectivity. Collaborating with various residents and stakeholders on the design, the students were urged to push the public standards toward equitable and pioneering solutions for the housing crisis. The studio underlined the importance of sustainability, resilience, and wellness (defined as cognitive, physical, and emotional well-being) as integral parts of the proposed solutions. Students were encouraged to reach beyond the expected tried-and-true strategies toward ambitious and visionary yet believable solutions.

2 Sadef Ali Kully, "Understanding NYCHA's New Rescue Plan," citylimits.org.

Interventions would include but not be limited to the following programs: housing, community and recreational spaces (amenities such as Laundromats, childcare centers, gyms, and multipurpose event spaces), as well as educational facilities, retail premises, parks, playgrounds, and parking areas. The students' proposals considered the replacement of existing buildings with new construction (as justified by a "best-use-of-land" argument), building infill (on open corners and between buildings), and improvements and additions to existing buildings.

Nnenna Lynch, the Bass Fellow, brought to the studio her expertise in socially responsible development. As a New Yorker with 18 years of work experience in development and public policy, Lynch has an unusual perspective on the studio's challenges. She informed the architectural investigations with an understanding of the necessary policy parameters and financial mechanisms to enable the successful realization of pioneering mixed-use and housing developments. Students benefited from her intimate understanding of New York City, experience on the NYCHA board, position as a Senior Policy Advisor in the Bloomberg administration leading transformational projects, and current focus through her firm, Xylem, on social and economic mobility as much as housing production.

Prior to embarking on the project, the students began with a short exercise that allowed them to reflect on low- and mixed-income housing in their hometowns as a way to calibrate a more concrete understanding. This was followed by brief research conducted in groups of three to four students to examine housing typologies, both international and domestic, over time and outline the successes and failures.

Travel week took the class to New York City and Los Angeles, where they visited a variety of housing developments. The East and West Coasts served as counterpoints demonstrating distinctly different solutions to low-income and affordable housing that respond to different cultures, climates, and contexts. During the trip to New York City the class visited the Tenement Museum as well as various NYCHA developments to form a baseline understanding of predominant conditions and particularities. The students engaged with resident representatives and NYCHA management and attended talks by leading figures in the world of housing policy and development. The trip to Los Angeles allowed the class to explore the possibilities offered by lower-density housing in terms of auxiliary programming and community-building spaces.

The aim of the studio was to rethink the housing formula and propose innovative ways for the architecture and mixed-use programming of low-income and affordable housing to embrace new approaches and create models for inclusive and equitable development in the city.

A Conversation about Affordable Housing and Design

Hana Kassem
Nnenna Lynch
Heather Roberge
James von Klemperer

The discussion on teaching and affordable housing was organized by Nina Rappaport with visiting professors Hana Kassem, Nnenna Lynch, and Jamie von Klemperer. Los Angeles architect Heather Roberge, who was also teaching an advanced studio as the Davenport Visiting Professor about housing, joined the discussion.

Nina Rappaport
Your studios focused on affordable housing and the housing crisis through exploring different forms, capacities, programs, and systems such as modular prefabrication in Los Angeles and the more permanent construction of New York City's public-housing infrastructure. Why did you each choose a specific approach, and what are the issues for public housing in general?

Hana Kassem
The focus of the studio, "Housing Redux," was how to recenter the conversation about low-income housing around the needs of residents

KPF, Eastern Red Hook Houses, Brooklyn: Power plant with boiler room and food retail visible at the base; a mural created by members of the community takes a central place at street level.

and how a development such as Washington Houses could contribute to the context of East Harlem. My coteachers and I, Nnenna, Jamie, and Andrei Harwell, focused the students on addressing issues of permanence, maintenance, and the sense of ownership (or the lack thereof) faced within New York City Housing Authority (NYCHA) developments. The deferred maintenance of the apartments is estimated at $40 billion. Many people age in apartments that are too big for them and don't know whether they will be guaranteed a suitable apartment if they agree to move to a smaller unit to allow for maintenance and repairs. There is a lot of distrust in the system. So the question of permanence was central to the students' evaluation of the Washington Houses, as were concepts for renewal through new programs and community spaces. The studio was organized in three parts: a review of low-income developments the students grew up around or encountered in their travels, research on housing precedents, and a two-part design problem. They developed a master plan framework in groups of three, adding 350 units and other programs to the development. The students were allowed to propose tearing down existing buildings as long as they replaced them with new housing of equal or greater capacity or with essential community spaces. During the second part of the studio, students worked individually on a variety of topics, from innovative housing to community and auxiliary spaces.

KPF, Red Hook Houses, Brooklyn: Aerial collage depicting the new resiliency flood-protection landscaping, electricity infrastructure, and distribution.

Nnenna Lynch

Housing is a foundational part of people's lives and a key determinant of life outcomes, so if you're interested in the principles of equality and opportunity, it's a critical piece of the picture. It is also essential from a community-planning perspective, that is when you think about land use, neighborhoods and urban revitalization. I started my career in East Harlem developing smaller-scale projects then went on to work in the Mayor's Office on a variety of issues including housing and later served on the board of NYCHA and more recently founded a mission-driven real estate company so I've been involved many facets of housing production, policy and public-private partnerships.

Heather Roberge

Issues of unmet housing needs, rising housing costs, and anticipated climate migration influenced the prefabricated housing studio "Climate Caravan," which I taught with Daisy Ames. Other influences were Bruno Latour's book *Down to Earth* and the film *Nomadland*, directed by Chloe Zhao and based on the book by Jessica Bruder. I watched the film from my pandemic headquarters, my family room, while the sky was orange from the wildfires raging 80 miles to the east, in Los Angeles. During this doubly apocalyptic scene, I pondered what it means to tackle the problem of housing in cities undergoing climate change and facing even greater climatic challenges in the future. One example was a recent competition called "Low-Rise Housing Ideas for Los Angeles," organized by Christopher Hawthorne, of the Los Angeles mayor's office, which solicited architects, landscape designers, and urbanists to produce ideas promoting "housing affordability, new paths to homeownership, and innovative models of sustainable residential architecture" by adding lots zoned for single-family use. In the studio we proposed to answer the following questions: How can we address the housing-supply deficit with portable housing infrastructure in cities like Los Angeles, at the top of the FEMA list of those most vulnerable to natural disaster? Can we densify a city like Los Angeles using prefabricated mass production so that people can be easily relocated to more hospitable climates in the future?

Nina Rappaport
The two studio topics integrate many currents, from housing shortages to climate change. Why this switch in focus for you in the Bass Studios, Jamie, from commercial residential design programs to pressing issues of public housing?

Jamie von Klemperer
Over the past 15 years we have been working at KPF on a wide range of residential projects in a variety of scales as well as social and urban contexts. An important goal of this studio was to explore the relationship of housing to other, complementary uses. We encouraged the idea of mixed-use residential typologies, proposing

to reinforce communities through integrated urban design. Rather than viewing NYCHA housing as inert and homogeneous, we looked at mixing different kinds of public and affordable housing, and even introducing market-rate products as financial levers for change. Added funding could unlock opportunities to provide desperately needed maintenance and improve the lives of the more than 500,000 residents of New York City public housing. There is clearly a movement today in both the profession and academia focused on making architecture serve the broadest range of people in society.

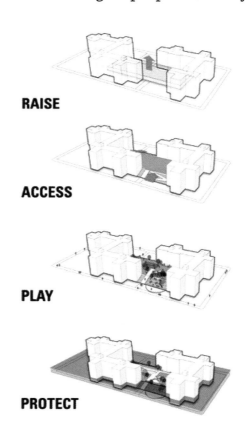

RAISE

ACCESS

PLAY

PROTECT

KPF, Red Hook Houses, Brooklyn: The "Lily-Pads," a landscape-based flood-protection strategy that enhances the day-to-day life of the residents by providing outdoor social spaces and new playgrounds.

It's hard to find a subject more relevant to the challenge of social betterment than NYCHA housing. Since the Bass Studio is focused on the benefits of introducing a developer's thinking into the design process, the opportunity to work with Nnenna on promoting positive change was really compelling. We all felt as if we were embracing a shared mission, both professionally and personally. As students we were exposed to foundational models of Modernist housing and saw that the legacy those ideas bestowed on U.S. cities was often seriously flawed. Nnenna and Hana came up with the title of the class, "Housing Redux," implying the need to reconsider public housing as a live building type and a social opportunity rather than merely a formula from the past.

Nina Rappaport
Hana, you have been working with KPF on NYCHA's Red Hook Houses, financed with FEMA funds, to make a more resilient residential complex. How did that project change the way NYCHA has been addressing housing issues?

Hana Kassem
Our work on recovery for the Red Hook Houses after Hurricane Sandy was limited to what the superstorm had impacted or preventative measures toward climate resiliency. The scope did not include solving NYCHA's deferred maintenance issues, with the exception of repairs to damaged roofs. We focused mostly on the spaces between the buildings. This was an infrastructure project that

included two new power plants and flood-protection measures designed as terraced landscaped courtyards, affording the residents a sense of community through new playgrounds and public spaces for each building cluster. NYCHA asked us to look at other scenarios separately from the FEMA-funded project. We studied improved vertical transport with elevators that access the top floor (currently this is not the case), proper egress, and a facade-cladding system to address the issue of uninsulated building envelopes and windows, among other scenarios. We hope these additional studies will be useful for other developments with similar conditions, although for funding reasons they could not be implemented at Red Hook Houses.

Nina Rappaport
How did you approach the residents to find out their needs, and were you able to actually apply these findings to other NYCHA projects?

Hana Kassem
NYCHA organized a number of town hall meetings at the Red Hook Houses for the residents to share their needs and for us to present our design propositions. We then identified areas of the development that needed improved lighting and sight lines for safety and water management, among other issues. The feedback informed our design priorities. NYCHA also organized workshops and focus groups with people interested in housing at the Center for Architecture, cohosted by the AIANY,

where we investigated measures such as "performative" landscapes, the building envelope, potential new buildings and infill, and how to leverage NYCHA's assets, namely property and grounds with very low density. A new RFP has been issued for the NYCHA Chelsea-Elliott and Fulton sites, and it is the first to be formulated directly out of a community-engagement process through resident workshops. KPF has remained involved in this work because it is critical to issues of equity in architecture.

Nina Rappaport
So it's really a master-planning framework for all of NYCHA that includes the residents for the first time.

Hana Kassem
Framework is a really good term for it because the solutions are not applicable everywhere, and each NYCHA development has a different population profile, cultural identity, topographic condition, density, and level of integration with the city grid.

Nina Rappaport
Heather, how do you see ideas developing for more flexible prefabricated housing versus frameworks for large-scale urban housing projects, and what did your students explore in terms of both the specific project and generic aspects?

Heather Roberge
We asked the students to design housing systems as modular components with variable configurations capable of responding to different sites. They were to test the organizational capacities of these systems on three sites a prototypical Los Angeles R-1 lot of 7,500 square feet, two adjacent R-1 lots of 15,000 square feet, and a brownfield site of 64 acres. Seventy-five percent of Los Angeles's land dedicated to housing is zoned as R-1 for single-family development. To address the lack of affordable housing, the city and state have altered zoning to allow for an incremental transformation of these lots. The 64-acre parcel is owned by a commercial entity, which gave students an opportunity to plan more expansive distributions of housing systems on one site. Designing for mobility meant that housing would occupy a site for 20 years, instead of 80 to 120, before moving to a new place. By designing for prefabrication, we had to consider transportation and material constraints for initial assembly and disassembly under migratory pressure.

Nina Rappaport
Have you been working in prefabrication, and how has it assisted with the desperate housing-supply situation since COVID-19?

Heather Roberge
I'm working on a prefabricated ADU in my office now and am interested in understanding how standard production and manufacturing techniques can

inspire architectural investigation and design ingenuity more broadly. There's been an incredible investment in the prefab industry over the last ten years by technology companies with an abundance of capital. This investment trend inspired two questions: Can we leverage prefab technology to lower the cost of housing? If so, what new social arrangements can follow? Recent prefab experiments haven't lowered the cost of housing substantially because everyone's trying to approach the problem through mass customization instead of thinking about how seriality drives costs down, mainly through repetition, material economy, and speed. We focused on these production-related questions in support of broader social ambitions and a desire for climate-adaptive responses to an unmet housing supply. The current unmet need of seven million units can't be met quickly without radically rethinking production and affordability.

Nina Rappaport
It is almost a critique of the NYCHA housing plan, where the buildings exemplify seriality. Hana, what did you ask your students to address in terms of making NYCHA housing more specific to its users?

Hana Kassem
The idea of sameness versus customization was very central to the studio. We urged the students to tackle issues of identity, community, and individuality. The repetition of systems—such

as brick with punched windows on towers, an undifferentiated way of meeting the ground plane, and no urban front—does not engage with the urban fabric and isolates people, creating "islands of otherness." The homogeneity of language pulls all of the NYCHA developments together under a single "visual signifier" while separating them from the urban context. The self-organized residents of Washington Houses tried to claim their habitat by creating gardens specific to their cultures, such as the "Trinidad" and "Puerto Rico" gardens. The ability to celebrate their differences and have an impact on their surroundings gave residents a sense of empowerment and belonging. Questions of seriality, homogeneity, and repetition came up a lot during the semester. Yet there was the sense that something customizable, and thus not associated with low-income housing, could be affordable due to a sheer quantity of units, where repetition makes almost anything economically feasible. Some students envisioned NYCHA building its own prefabrication factory to unlock the potential for large-scale customized design.

Nina Rappaport
What amenities did the students include on the NYCHA site, and where do you think their design work and creativity was best applied?

Jamie von Klemperer
There was really a wide range. The Washington Houses gave the students a body on which to operate, rather than a fresh brief

for a completely new building. The resulting projects varied from landscape designs and public functions such as libraries, fitness centers, and shared food facilities to facade alterations and ways for families of different sizes and generations to move through NYCHA housing. If we had limited ourselves strictly to what can be built tomorrow, there wouldn't have been enough room for students to exercise their imaginations. At the same time we felt we needed to ask that the projects adhere to the realities of notional cost, zoning, and demographics. The studio had an inherent ethic, and we strove to help the students find the right balance between practicality and vision.

Nina Rappaport
Nnenna, do you think there was increased pragmatism because you were teaching as the Bass Fellow in a so-called "developer" studio?

Nnenna Lynch
I do think the role of a Bass Fellow is geared toward pragmatism, and for this studio a critical piece of that was understanding and respecting the existing context and its residents. One of the unique things about the studio was the immediacy of the issues, so it didn't feel like it was an entirely academic or theoretical exercise. Washington Houses is made up of 1,500 units and accommodates generations of families. We met with residents to instill in the students a respect for the people who live there. Yet while trying to impart a certain

level of pragmatism, we encouraged creativity—and balancing the two is one of the challenges of a studio like this. It's a constant tension that we've discussed explicitly.

Nina Rappaport
It is interesting that each studio traveled to Los Angeles to see housing projects. Heather, your site was there, so what did you visit for inspiration?

Heather Roberge
The Los Angeles trip was designed as a kind of genealogical study of housing experiments across time and types. We visited an early tilt-up concrete housing site by Irving Gill, bungalow courts built in response to rapid population growth in the early nineteenth century, Gregory Ain's Mar Vista tract, and Case Study homes that offered new spatial arrangements for the nuclear family. We visited recent prefab housing developments by Michael Maltzan as well as a series of prefab production facilities. Students saw firsthand how architects have addressed the production of housing creatively while learning how the projects were informed by both ideas and a particular sociopolitical context.

Nina Rappaport
Jamie, why did you travel to Los Angeles to do research for a site in New York?

Jamie von Klemperer
The pandemic didn't allow us to go to Copenhagen, London, or Berlin, so we turned to the West Coast as an alternative. The context there

KPF, Red Hook Houses, Brooklyn: Electric distribution pods anchor each cluster of buildings, contributing to a sense of identity and security through color and lighting.

engenders a sense of freedom, and architects are drawn to its spirit of experimentation. Since Los Angeles is not as dense as New York and the land values are not as prohibitive, the setting allows for more flexibility. Low-rise buildings and mild weather allow more possibilities for outdoor circulation. Exposure to Los Angeles precedents also freed the students to break away from the more rigid NYCHA context. I think they were really inspired by some of the beautiful earlier works of Richard Neutra and Rudolph Schindler. During our tours we tried to understand the specific issues of cost, social demographics, and local regulations. In one of the recent affordable-housing projects we saw, the cost per unit was a sobering $500,000. Housing law and funding conspired to create this kind of budget, but it's clearly not a sustainable equation. This anomaly pointed out that though there is a national need for public housing, the problems that architects need to solve vary widely from city to city. Among the projects we visited, the work of Koning Eizenberg made an especially strong impression on the students and provided great examples of how to use modest materials to make beautiful spaces.

Nina Rappaport
Architects are often left out of housing design and planning. Heather, how does the age-old question of whether or not design should have more of a role in both public and market-rate housing play out today?

Heather Roberge
When architects are designing only two percent of U.S. housing, we know

that production economics drive the marketplace. When housing supply doesn't meet demand, costs rise. In the United States wages have remained flat while housing costs have grown exponentially. The growth in the value of housing as an asset and personal wealth that homeownership generates leaves far too many people without shelter. The book *Evicted*, written by Matthew Desmond, chronicles the experiences of property owners and their often economically disadvantaged tenants. The author addresses the deferred maintenance that accompanies housing subsidized by public funding and the poor quality of the resulting environments, which Hana mentioned. Subsidies don't correct the supply problem and simply provide yet another avenue for profit taking. The fact that housing is an instrument for profit rather than a human right is a major societal problem. Architects do not write economic policy, but they can respond to production constraints and material economies in the delivery of affordable projects. We can address issues of repetition, technology, and labor, all of which impact housing. Architects can also anticipate future need and the social impact of spatial organization. How do people live and with whom? How do these social arrangements change over time? What social models have people adopted to manage housing costs? The students used these questions to incorporate adaptability into their housing systems and site arrangements.

Nina Rappaport
Is the cost of design getting in the way of affordable housing? Nnenna, how do you see the role of design in housing?

Nnenna Lynch
The key to achieving effective, well-designed low-cost housing depends on the skills and commitment of your design team. Budgets create constraints, but there is a deep community of architects who embrace them as points of departure for creativity, inventiveness, and thoughtfulness. In the history of affordable housing there has been a big shift from a focus on no-frills unit production, something that is replicable, to an appreciation for the power of design. The key to that shift is thoughtful, creative, and pragmatic designers.

Hana Kassem
We also have to realize that what we build impacts people in both positive and negative ways. So it is not just "nice" to have good design but a basic human right because it affects well-being and health. In that sense designers, architects, and planners can have a huge impact on social equity and quality of life. In videos shared by residents of the Washington Houses, people said, "I want to be part of something beautiful, something that makes me feel good."

Nina Rappaport
The implementation of affordable housing is, of course, political. How can architects and developers convince policymakers to institute a national

regulation that decrees housing as a basic right equal to infrastructural systems like roads and bridges?

Heather Roberge

It's enormously difficult to steer the ship. Take California's recent State Bill 9 as an example. It addresses affordability and supply by allowing single-family lots to double in unit density. Other legislation effectively quadruples the number of units allowed on these parcels. After Governor Gavin Newsom survived a recent recall election, he signed SB9 as part of an ambitious plan to deliver statewide housing units at 30 times the current annual rate. Immediately thereafter the Los Angeles city council voted overwhelmingly to fight the legislation in court because many voters have something to lose. Some fear a loss of property value and neighborhood character, while others are afraid the financial incentives of development will lead to more gentrification, tenant displacement, and lack of affordability. The *New York Times* recently published an opinion piece by Ezra Klein reporting on the importance of inventive approaches to the supply of housing. He discusses the unintended consequences of public-housing subsidies, such as rising home costs due to increasing demand. The studio examined this complex issue while recognizing its many facets.

Nnenna Lynch

Developers influence policy through doing business and participating in local and national organizations and forums. One of the challenges of housing is that it's an insular realm, and a lot of the policy discussions relate to fairly arcane rules and regulations. The events of this past year have emphasized the importance of housing and its shortcomings in relation to the larger body politic. I believe architects have a big role to play because the constraints require real creativity to resolve the issues. Developers can't do it alone, and architects are key partners in using limited resources to create something special. We can talk about different housing typologies or building methodologies and how to be efficient with resources, but to solve the housing crisis we really need additional funding and subsidies.

Jamie von Klemperer

Architects often feel that they have very little agency to affect policy because they are at the bottom of the food chain in terms of money and power. So it's important to realize that we are actually at the top when it comes to ideas—architectural propositions can be really powerful. In this studio we did not ask students to introduce revolutionary new paradigms that would completely reshape the practice. Instead we suggested that progress is incremental and that investigating affordable-housing typologies and solutions can help stir the pot and get people thinking in transformative directions. Students were encouraged to propose changes both to the configurations of dwelling spaces and to the public realm, including landscape areas, streetscapes, and roof surfaces.

WASHINGTON

HOUSES

The site proposed for the studio is the NYCHA Washington Houses, in East Harlem, otherwise known as Spanish Harlem or El Barrio. One of the largest predominantly Hispanic communities in New York City (52.1%), it is home to vibrant communities with roots in Puerto Rico, the Dominican Republic, Cuba, and Mexico. The Black population represents the second-largest minority group, at 35.7 percent. Historically East Harlem has suffered from a number of social, security, and health issues such as high rates of crime, joblessness, homelessness, drug abuse, and teenage pregnancy, an AIDS epidemic, and five times more cases of severe asthma than the national average due to pollution inequity.[3] Poor economic development and planning has led to a lack of access to healthy food for residents of East Harlem.[4] It is one of the areas of the city with the highest levels of diet-related diseases due to limited opportunities for citizens to purchase fresh foods.[5]

In the 1950s and '60s large sections of East Harlem, which had been redlined by the Home Owners Loan Corporation in 1938, were leveled for urban-renewal projects. The neighborhood was one of the hardest hit in terms of social and economic issues in the 1960s and '70s while New York City struggled with budget deficits, race riots, gang warfare, drug abuse, crime, poverty, and urban flight. Tenements were crowded, poorly maintained, and frequent targets for arson. The area has the second-highest concentration of public housing in the United States.

Washington Houses encompasses the equivalent of seven city blocks between Second and Third Avenues, from 97th Street to 104th Street. Consolidated into three megablocks, the project is accessed only by streets passing through at East 99th and 102nd Streets. The "houses"— cruciform towers that are 14 stories tall on average—are rotated to a true north-south orientation, ignoring the city grid, with curving paths that weave between the buildings to connect the development. The housing towers, comprising a total of 1,511 units, cover only 13.9 percent of the land area, so there is plenty of opportunity for redevelopment.[6]

One of the distinguishing features of the development is its generous landscaping, including a central circular garden. Washington Houses is relatively well maintained, partly due to the residents' sense of ownership and empowerment. The neighboring El Barrio Artspace PS109 is a renowned community-driven arts facility that has transformed an abandoned public high school with 90 units of affordable live/work housing for artists and their families, as well as space for various art organizations.

3 PACT, https://www1.nyc.gov/site/nycha/about/pact.page
4 Eating in East Harlem: https://cunyurbanfoodpolicy.org/resources/report/eating-in-east-harlem
5 Ibid.
6 Ibid.

Welcome Sign

Tower View

Tower Facades

Garden Areas

Seating Area

Site Community Garden

Recreation Area

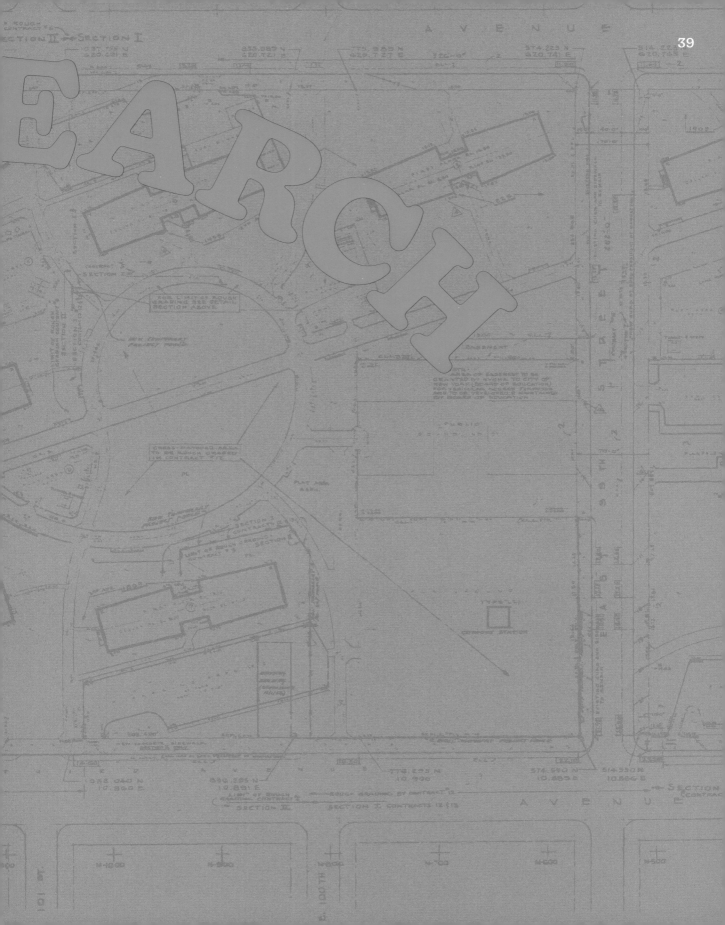

Case Studies

For the first assignment of the studio's research phase, students were given a list of possible case studies and selected one contemporary and one historical project to analyze. They were asked to investigate historical, socio-economic and political context, demographics, programming and planning, dimensions and scale, materiality and language, as well as any salient features or notable innovations in the housing typology.

1871
Peabody Estates
London, UK

1927–30
Karl Marx Hof
Vienna, Austria

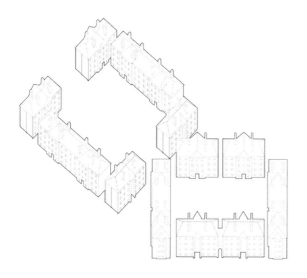

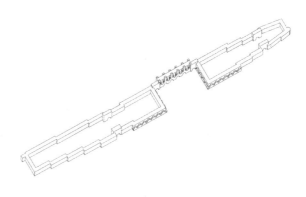

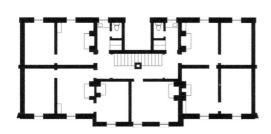

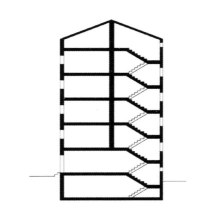

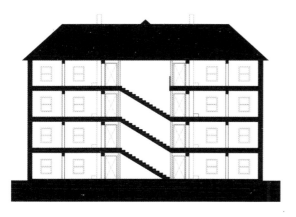

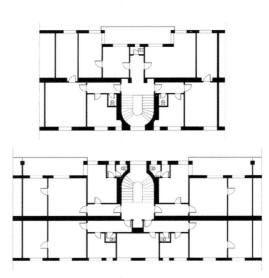

1928
Wohnstadt Carl Legien
Berlin, Germany

1947
Unite d'Habitation
Marseilles, France

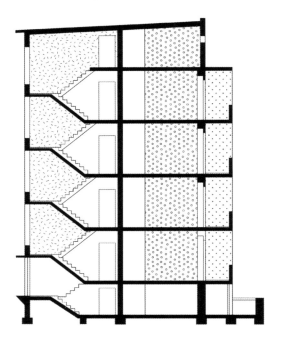

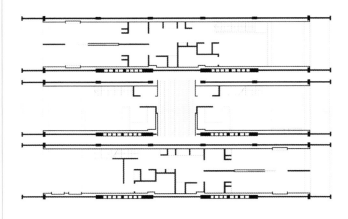

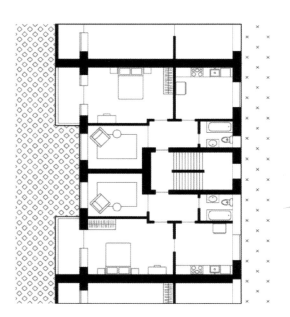

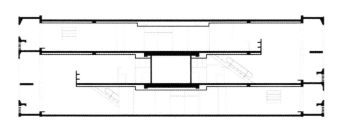

1969–82
Byker Wall Estate
Newcastle Upon Tyne, UK

1972
Trellick Tower
London, UK

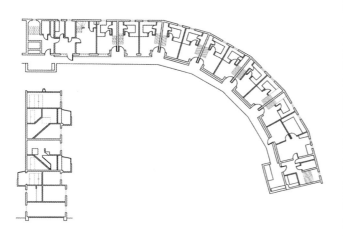

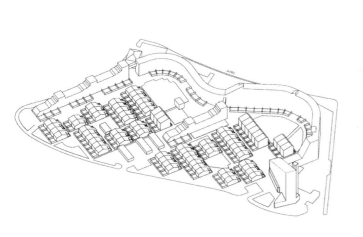

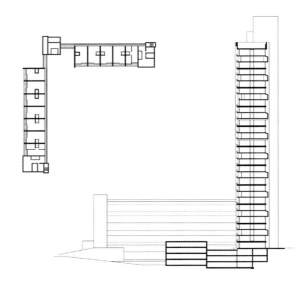

2000
Plaza Cerdá Housing
Barcelona, Spain

2005
Tietgen Dormitory
Copenhagen, Denmark

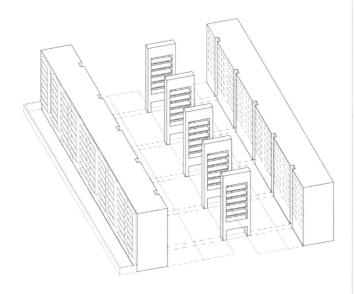

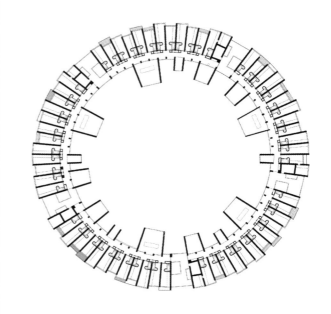

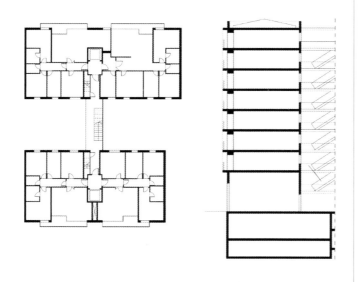

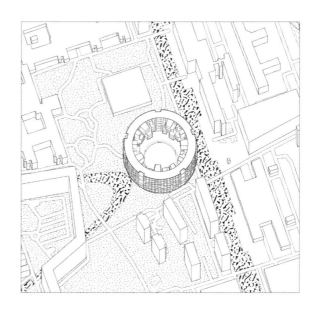

2008
The Mountain Dwellings
Copenhagen, Denmark

2014
Heliópolis Social Housing
São Paulo, Brazil

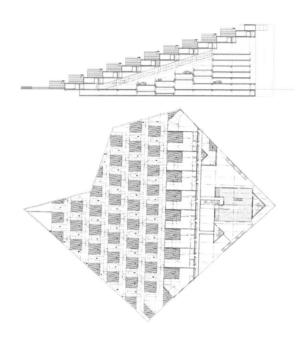

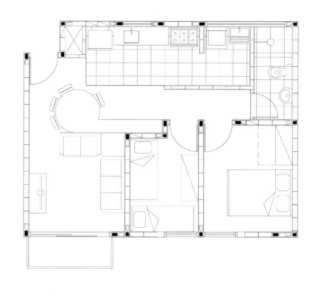

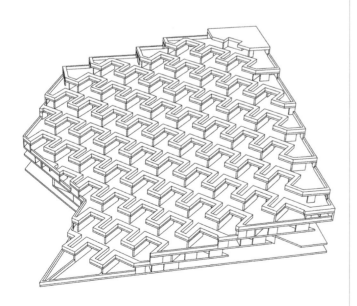

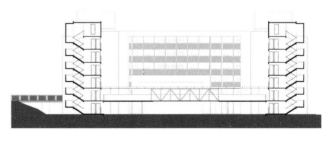

2015
Star Apartments
Los Angeles, California

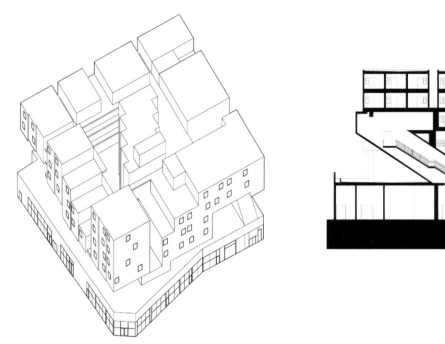

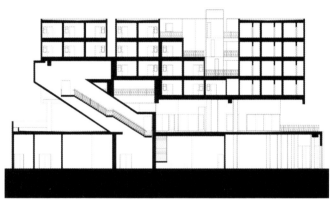

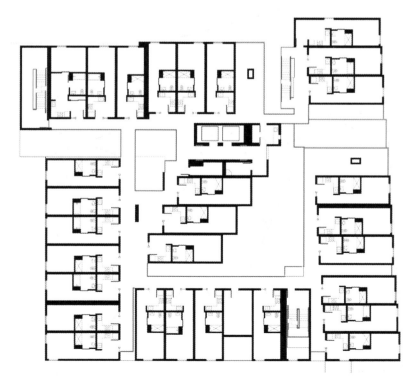

2017
Drivelines Studios
Johannesburg, South Africa

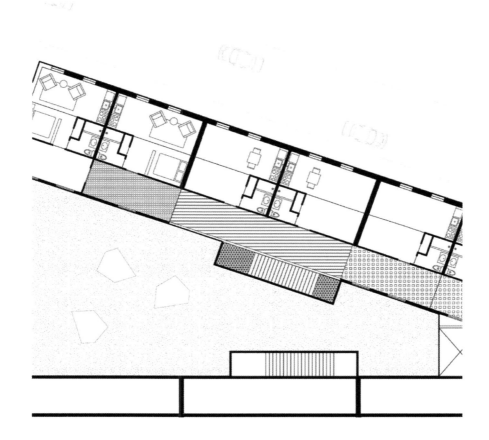

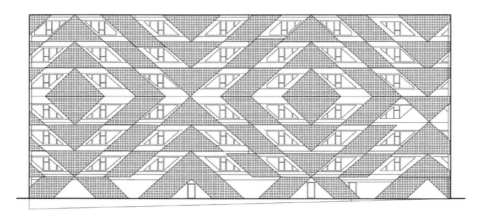

Initial Proposals

For the second assignment, students were to reflect on their site visit and provide a preliminary conceptual argument for programmatic and design concepts for Washington Houses, supported by analysis, visual material, and diagrams. Within their proposals, they outlined key program elements for a master-plan framework, set density goals and a narrative, and defined sustainability, resiliency, and wellness goals.

Group 1
Claudia Ansorena
Vignesh Harikrishnan
Saba Salekfard

Group 2
Lindsay Duddy
Dominiq Oti
David Scurry

Group 3
Levi Shaw-Faber
Suhyun Jang
Raul Martiniez Martinez

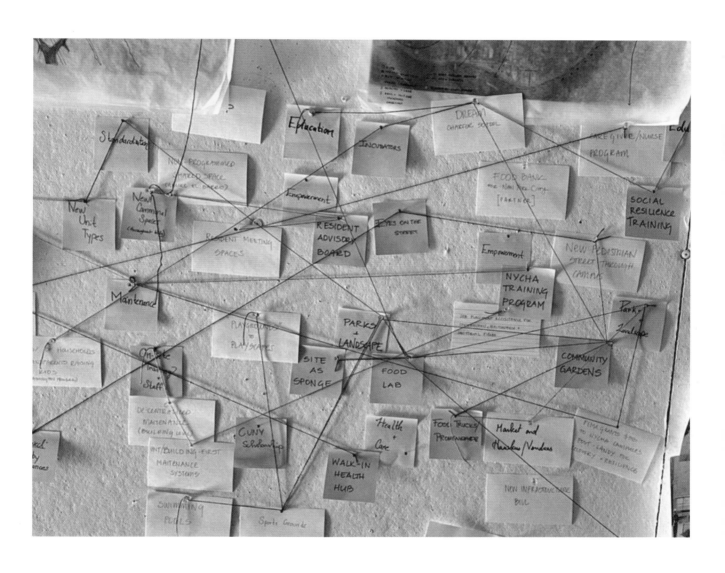

Project Research Map: Connecting Parts to the Whole

Group 1

NYCHA's Standardization Issue

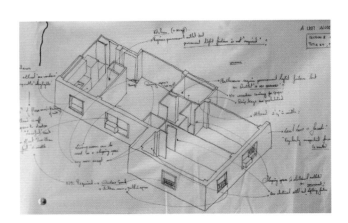

Landscape Site

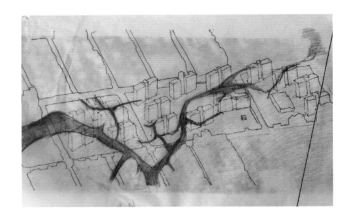

100-Year Flood Map

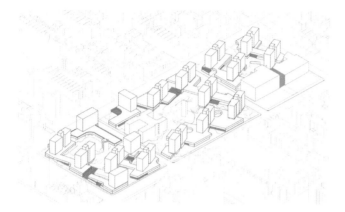

Utilizing In-Between Space Diagram

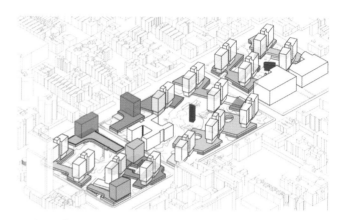

Project Phasing Diagram

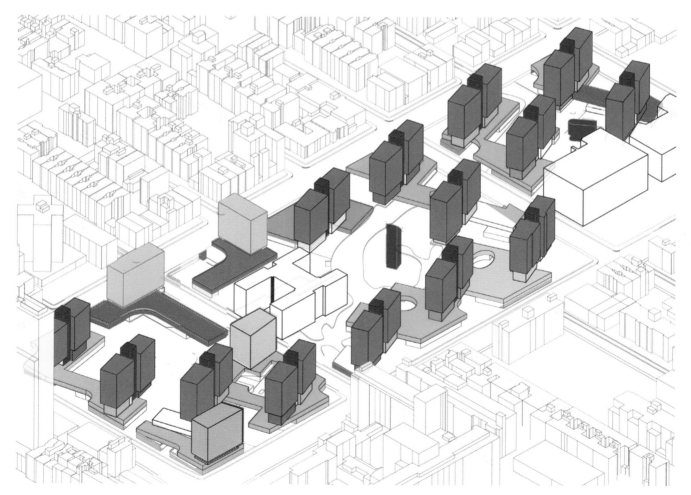

Proposed Program Diagram

Group 2

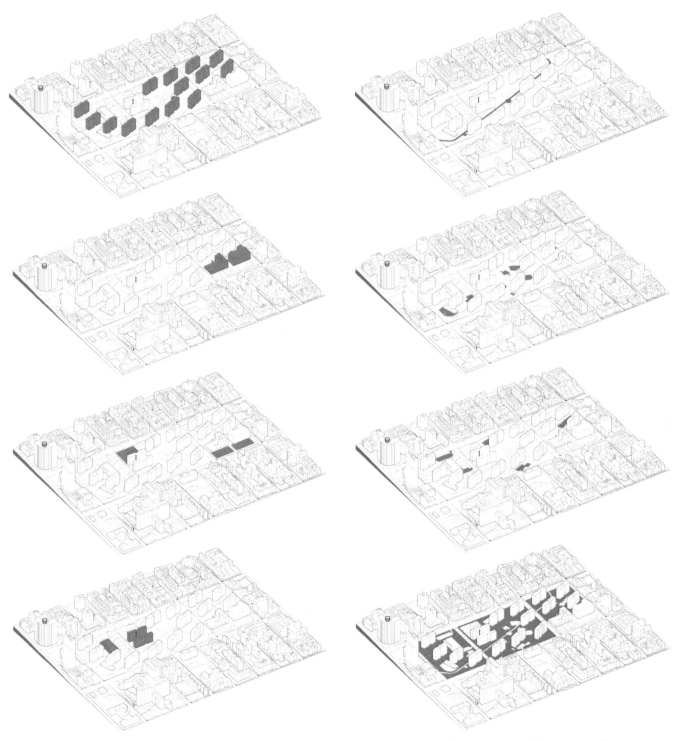

Project site assets include parks, schools, and social and cultural institutions.

Site issues include excessive parking, unusable open space, and obscured fenced areas.

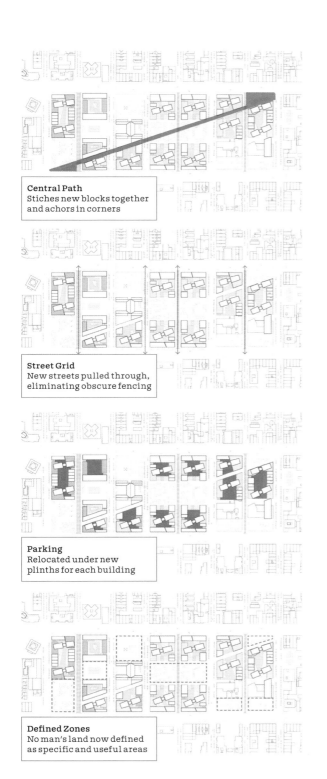

Central Path
Stiches new blocks together
and achors in corners

Street Grid
New streets pulled through,
eliminating obscure fencing

Parking
Relocated under new
plinths for each building

Defined Zones
No man's land now defined
as specific and useful areas

Site Proposals Diagrams

Site Asset Photographs

Group 3

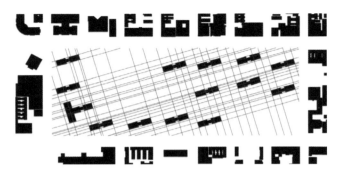
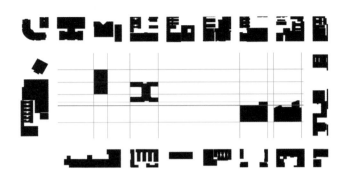

Figure Ground Study of Existing Site Grids

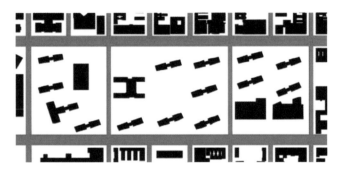

Existing Site versus Proposed Project Avenues

Proposed thoroughfares connect the project back to the city.

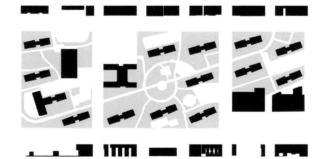
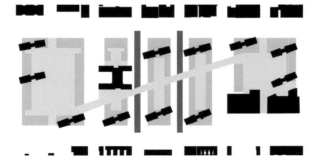

Proposed open green space is framed by the project's new architecture.

Unusable Open Space

Uninviting Fenced-in Areas

Master Plan Proposals

This studio aimed to envision new architectural solutions for NYCHA's Washington Houses development that address the city's housing shortage while tackling more general questions of urban fabric and context, public and private space, and mixed-use development as a tool for connectivity—as well as the economic challenges of deferred maintenance and shrinking municipal funds. Collaborating with residents and city agencies, students were urged to push the envelope to arrive at equitable and pioneering design solutions. Studio prompts emphasized the importance of sustainability, resiliency, and wellness (defined as cognitive, physical, and emotional well-being) as integral parts of the proposed solutions and as paths to equity in design.

With the above goals in mind, the students incorporated initial observations from their site visit in an outline for a mixed-use program that responded to the following minimum guidelines:

- Provide 350 to 550 new units on the site.

- Include various mixed-use programs, such as community spaces, Laundromats, childcare centers, gyms, multipurpose event spaces, retail premises, training and career centers, and cultural and arts spaces.

- Incorporate parks, playgrounds, and parking areas.

- Consider the replacement of existing buildings to open up possibilities for new construction (as justified by a "best-use-of-land" argument). If demolition of existing housing is proposed, a decanting scheme must be developed (i.e. units demolished need to be replaced in the first phase of a new build proposal).

- Consider including building infill (on open corners and between buildings).

- Consider a combination of high-rise and low-rise, or a mix of both.

- Consider improvements and additions to existing buildings, including recladding, upgrading of lobby spaces, vertical circulation, and new ground-floor uses.

Group 1

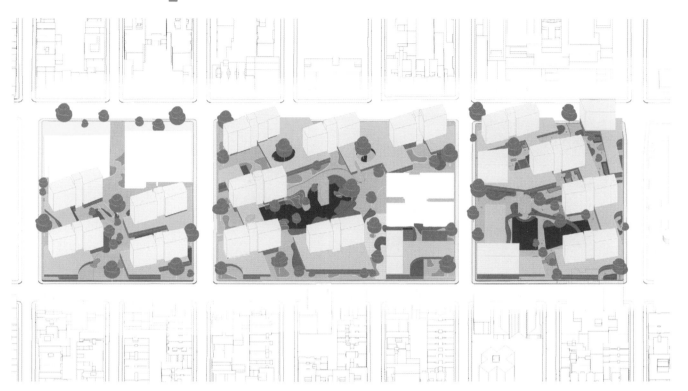

Master Plan Oblique

This is a project about weaving together and connecting the scales of urban life, from the living unit, building, and the site to the city. The project takes on notions of "mat urbanism," proposing instead a landscape urbanism focused on defined programming and an informal ground plane. Landscape and program are the unifying elements of the master plan. To encourage the fullest range of possibilities for encounters to take place, the project used landscape and development of the public realm to create a series of scripted and unscripted scenarios throughout the site. A series of objects dispersed around the site suggests an interplay between the designed elements and the intermediate events of the future. Thus transitional spaces become as important as the nodes they connect, producing woven and interlaced movement that connects to the city.

Here interstitial space creates opportunity for community gathering, provided by the new podium levels attached to the existing towers: landscape as building, landscape as urbanism, and program as form. Ultimately the proposal asked, What defines the field, the room, the building, or the city?

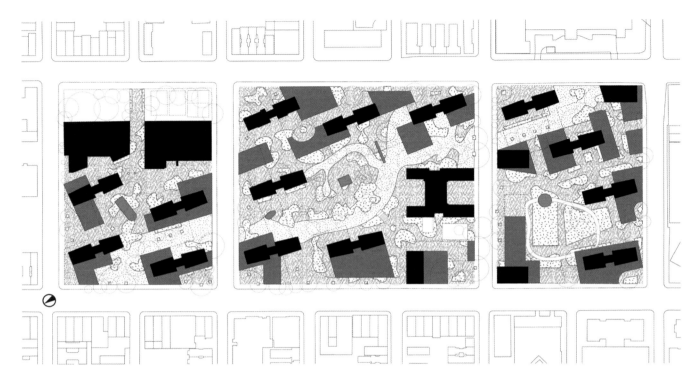

Master Plan Figure Ground

Master Plan Kit of Parts Diagram

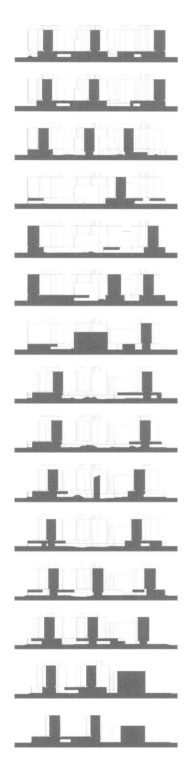

Serial Site Sections

View of Activated Ground Plane

View of Shared Public Spaces

Group 2

The aim of this project, titled "Reimagining Washington Houses," is to support NYCHA in its mission and reorganize the power dynamic between the landlord and tenant, giving more agency to residents by reintegrating them into the civic identity of East Harlem.

From our analysis we concluded that NYCHA represents an obscure system of authority and power that governs the lives of residents of its projects across New York City with limitations including a lack of resources, outdated housing models, a complex system of power dynamics, and a missing sense of ownership. The site of Washington Houses also faced spatial problems: the diagonal central path is curtailed at odd places, parking takes up potential space for other programmatic functions, and there are unoccupied fenced-in spaces in open areas. Thus the strategy for our master plan proposal was to address and offer solutions for each of these issues.

We chose to maintain the diagonal central path to stitch together new proposed blocks, having it terminate into two open gathering spaces that anchor the corners of the overall site. We connected the site to the existing street grid in East Harlem, allowing some streets to accommodate vehicles while reserving others entirely for pedestrians. Parking is relocated within the bases of the buildings, to be accessed from the avenue, so it no longer takes up valuable open space. We redefined the unprogrammed fenced green space into distinct areas that provide various types of outdoor environments for the community.

Given these proposed alterations, we could look at the overall site plan. The project proposes new housing aimed at diversifying the residential typology of the site by introducing low-rise density: 150,000 SF of town houses and 500,000 SF of apartments, all spread over massing of four to five floors. The new housing is arranged along the plan's new cross streets. Alongside the housing are new commercial buildings that fill out the urban fabric with facades along the avenues as a way to diversify a homogeneously programmed site. Thus the buildings form a more typical New York avenue rather than retreating from it. Lastly the proposal introduces new social spaces designed primarily for the NYCHA residents. The union settlement is relocated next to El Barrio with a public face to the street. The social space is combined with housing to accommodate a range of communal activities.

Newly defined green space anchors the two corners of the site: the central park reinforces a sense of belonging and a "community center" intended for a variety of recreational uses; a community pool, flanked on two sides by new

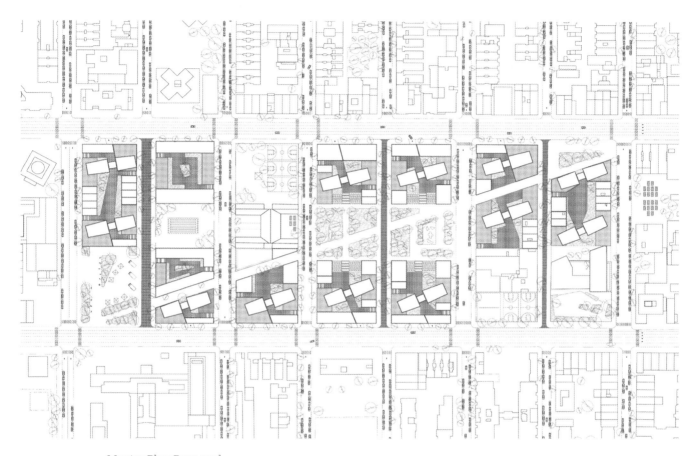

Master Plan Proposal

apartments, provides programmatic specificity. A food truck plaza serving the public and hospital staff reinforces the existing playgrounds facing the avenues.

Lastly, the project looked at typical unit configurations. It provides a middle level as an intervention to the tower and plinth, with parking underneath and access from

the avenue. Retail spaces face the avenue, and row houses face the street, spaced around plinths. New apartment blocks around the plinth connect to the parking space from the cores. The majority of the NYCHA tower will be kept in place, with part of the first four floors removed. Pedestrian access runs through the site via stairs from the street and to the planted steps.

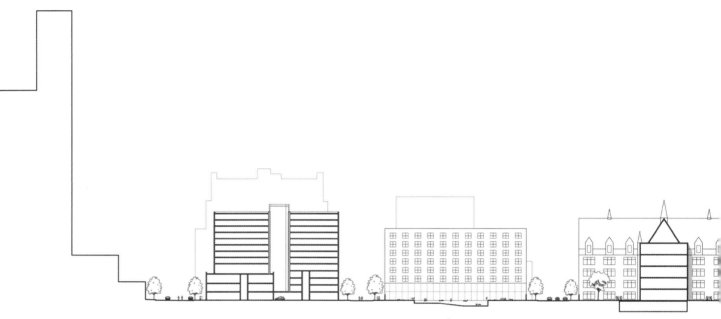

Site Section

Better-Defined Park Space

New Housing

Proposed Thoroughfare

Group 3

Our project, "Neighborhood Connections," focuses on reintegrating the city grid onto the site of Washington Houses by introducing new streets and public thoroughfares. The new streets allow diversification of housing options on the site and integrate low-rise typologies such as the row house alongside mid-rise residential buildings among the existing towers.

The project proposes a series of landscaped parks, linked by a green pathway running perpendicularly throughout site, to connect the new streets to the larger development. Lastly, new program types such as community spaces, greenhouses, and retail shops will be introduced to promote engagement among the residents and with the community at large.

Master Plan Proposal

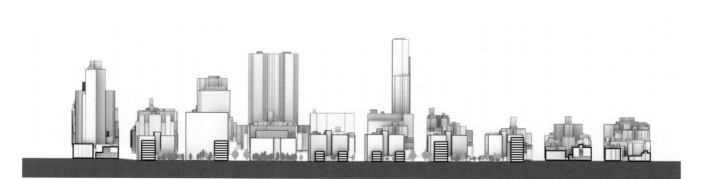

Longitudinal Site Section

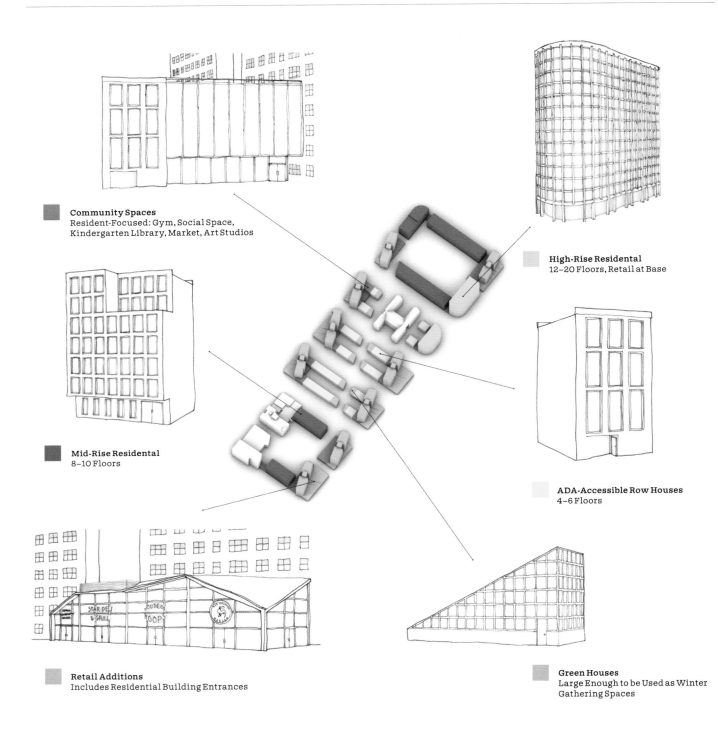

Community Spaces
Resident-Focused: Gym, Social Space,
Kindergarten Library, Market, Art Studios

High-Rise Residental
12–20 Floors, Retail at Base

Mid-Rise Residental
8–10 Floors

ADA-Accessible Row Houses
4–6 Floors

Retail Additions
Includes Residential Building Entrances

Green Houses
Large Enough to be Used as Winter
Gathering Spaces

Programmatic and Typology Diagram

Ground-View Perspective

Market Perspective

STUDENT WO

For the final project the professors asked students to develop a portion of their master plan proposals for the remainder of the semester. Students decided on the scope of the project and chose whether to work individually or stay within the designated groups. The results revealed a range of focus points, with proposals taking on a single building or the development of an entire block.

A Horizontal Urbanism
Claudia Ansorena
Vignesh Harikrishnan
Saba Salekfard

Reimagining Affordable Housing at Washington Houses
Lindsay Duddy

The Interspace: Weaving the Community
Suhyun Jang

Urban Reciprocity
Dominiq Oti

Here Comes the Sun
Raul Martinez Martinez

A Dancing Perimeter Block
David Scurry

Brownstone Reimagined
Levi Shaw-Faber

Horizontal Urbanism

Claudia Ansorena
Vignesh Harikrishnan
Saba Salekfard

NYCHA housing can be perceived as an impenetrable volume. It is stoic in nature and monotonous in its aggregate form. The individual gets lost in the system of identical brick facades. Following the intentions of the larger site-design framework, the project explores the individual within a collective body and further within the larger city. It tackles the tension and ambiguity of in-between spaces, such as lobbies, shared corridors, and stairs, and the structural elements between units, walls, and ceilings. The goal is to create diversity in program and form through the renovation of existing units at the scale of the unit and building, and its relationship to the street and city.

This is a project about cultivating the in-between, about extending the thresholds between people and place, home and community, individual and collective. It is a project about inscribing new traces and users without erasing history. It is about reinterpretations and reintroductions as well as giving importance to history by peeling back and through its layers. This project weaves and connects the scales of urban life, from the unit to the building and the site to the city beyond. The project is perceived through its parts, in a syntax of part-to-part relationships, where transitional spaces are just as important as the nodes they connect. We are designing for improvisational behavior to encourage freedom of movement and play. Here time is a dimension too; space is defined through functions and events, not always architecture; seasons emerge through landscapes, follies

adapt, programs shift, and spaces move. Meanwhile existing definitions of family, unit, home, and community are evoked by the current economic and political climate, to which opposition seems impossible, even if it were desirable. Standardized doors, handles, closets, and tenant profiles have been forced upon a market as an outcome of set conditions. It is challenging to manage or even question standardization when it serves other factors such as affordability, maintenance, ownership, and efficiency. However each of these factors represents an opportunity for optimization. This project questions the standardization of units through the lens of objects and the room, floor, building, person, family, community, and society. Rather than a one-size-fits-all master plan approach, which includes only minor optimizations at each scale, this project takes a bottom-up approach to redefine the standards with incisive partnership-led reconfigurations.

The home is expanded outside of itself, beyond the unit. The project reimagines NYCHA's tower-in-the-park typology and proposes a new collective model of high-rise living. It investigates the thresholds between the individual and the collective, and looks into connecting the unit to the community programming offered by the building and adjacent landscape, and everything in-between. How can shifts in the unit affect programming on the site, and vice versa? The project hopes to promote new communities and ways of living through this method by offering hybrid and informal programming.

A HORIZONTAL URBANISM

Welcome Home!

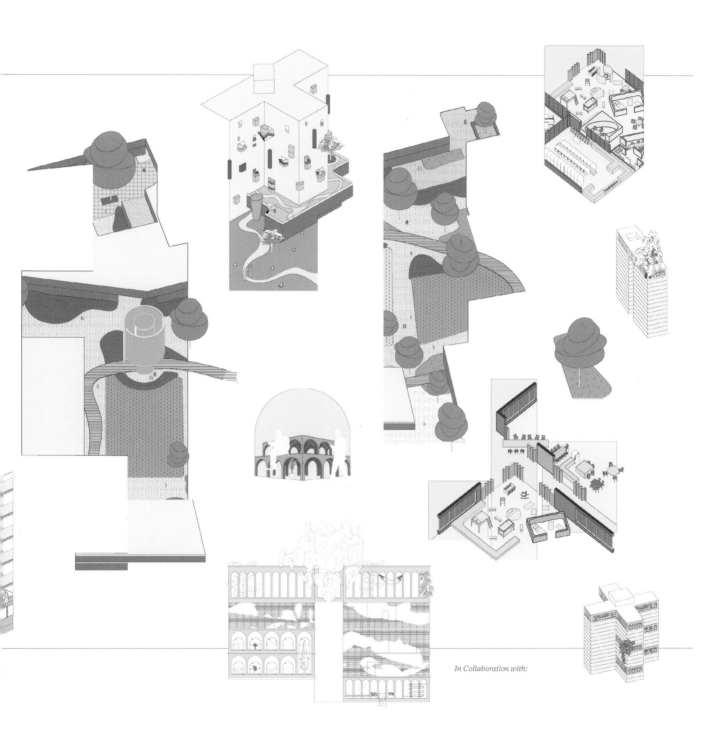

In Collaboration with:

Building Elevation

Floor-Level Isometric

Shared Common Spaces

Building Elevation Alternative

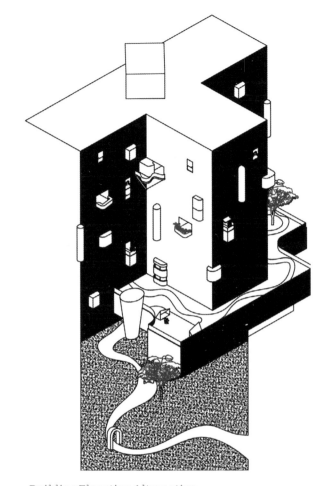

Building Elevation Alternative

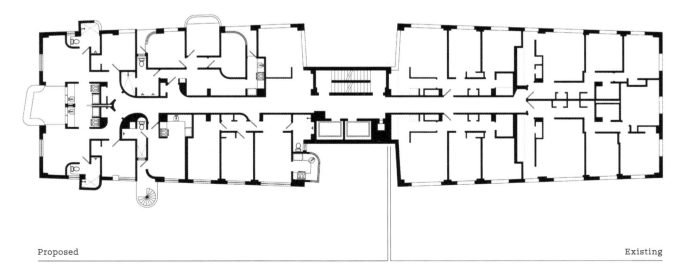

Proposed

Existing

Proposed Floor Plan

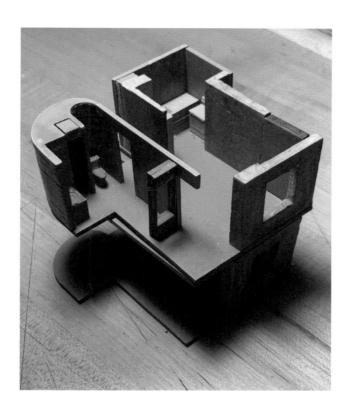

Model of Proposed Unit

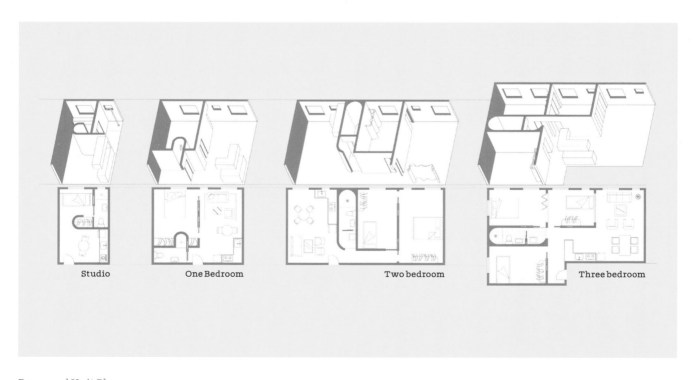

Studio   One Bedroom   Two bedroom   Three bedroom

Proposed Unit Plans

View from the Landscape Threshold Walls

View from the Housing

View from the Health and Wellness Spaces

View from the Educational Spaces

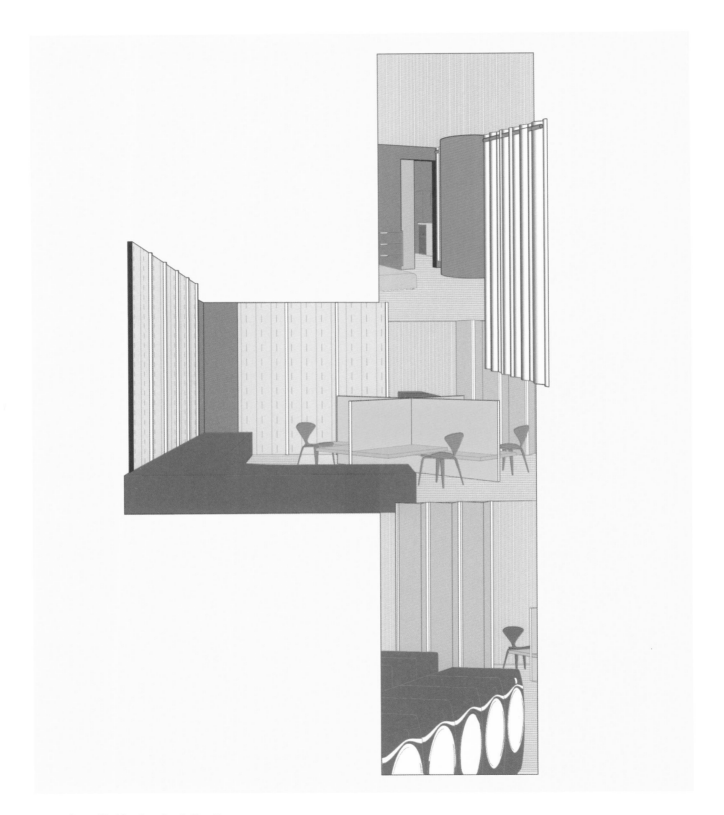

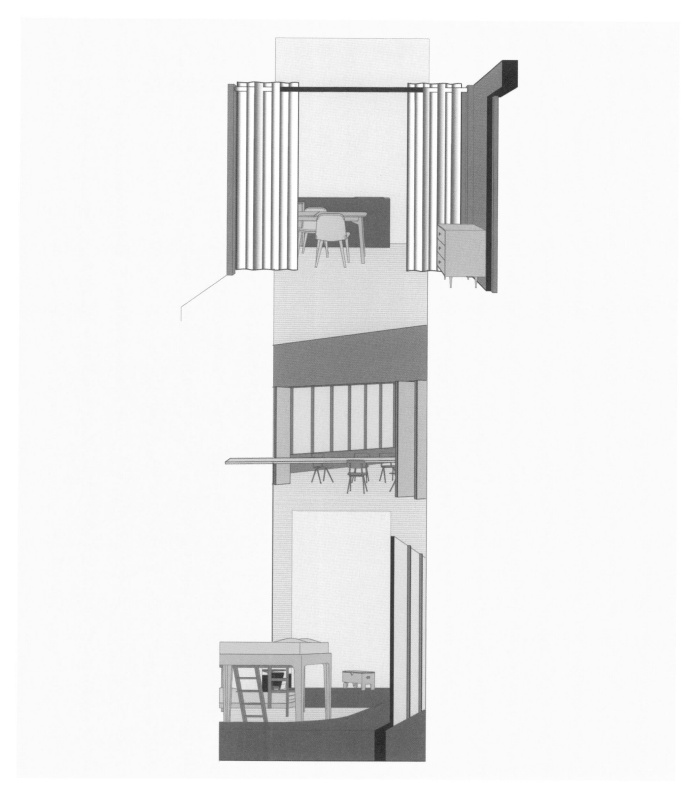

From the Private to the Public

Reimagining Affordable Housing at Washington Houses

An Ecological and Sustainable Community in the Heart of East Harlem

Lindsay Duddy

In 1934 New York City, plagued by a lack of affordable housing, created the New York City Housing Authority. This agency would utilize both local and federal resources for the construction and maintenance of high-rise affordable housing throughout the boroughs. Swaths of low-rise housing were cleared and replaced by campuses of austere identical brick buildings. They still stand today as they did then but are characterized by a general lack of maintenance. While the buildings require attention, it has become evident that the most critical need is a redesign of the spaces between the buildings and the relationship between the towers and their surroundings, which are neglected and underutilized. This project focused on designing public areas to create an ecological environment with a role in maintaining community-wide health and wellness.

The residents of Washington Houses are proud of their community, and close communal ties between neighbors create strong cross-cultural bonds. While the people create a community, the physical gathering spaces hindered their ability to interact. The campus reads as a maze of winding concrete paths lined on either side with iron fencing. These harsh, unwelcoming conditions leave residents with vast areas of inaccessible green spaces—a valuable asset in a dense city. The plots were gradually being used by the residents with minimal resistance from NYCHA. Small community gardens have sprouted up throughout the site, and residents share the produce. Mad Fun Farms, a city-based community gardening organization, also maintains a plot on the site to provide middle and high school students with an educational gardening experience.

This design project is centered around the consolidation of the site's ambiguous and atomized open space into a central park. The space was segmented into a series of community gardening plots, which can be leased to nonprofits or to the residents. The remaining space can be used for community functions, small gatherings, or exchange. One of the major architectural issues identified by the team during the master-planning phase was the way in which the current NYCHA building hits the ground. In an attempt to create varied zones of privacy, the exterior spaces expand onto the new elevated plinths, blending the spaces into one another. The entrances to the existing tower and new duplex units are accessed from the platform. This topological change allows for the perceived differentiation of spaces without the use of fences or other harsh barrier conditions.

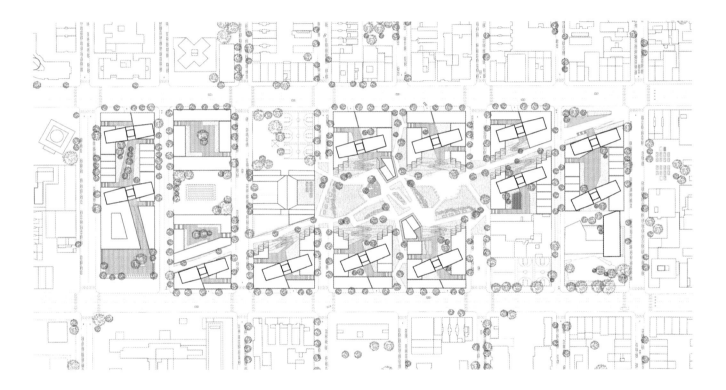

Master Plan

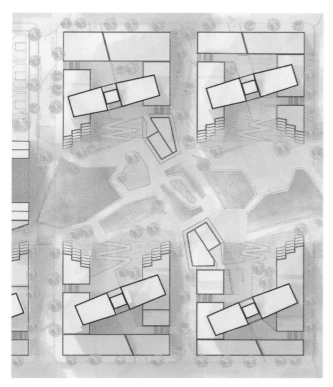

Central Plan

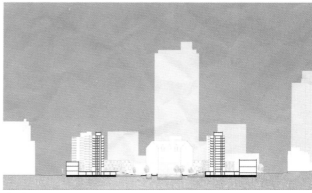

Section One

Section Two

Short Section

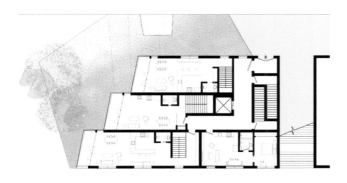

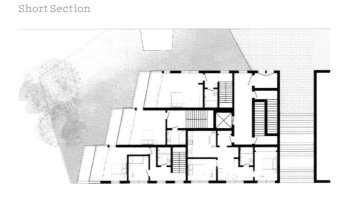

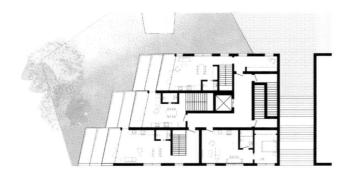

Apartments Floor Plan

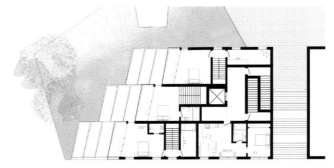

Master Plan View

Overall Site Model

View from the Housing

View from the Health and Wellness Spaces

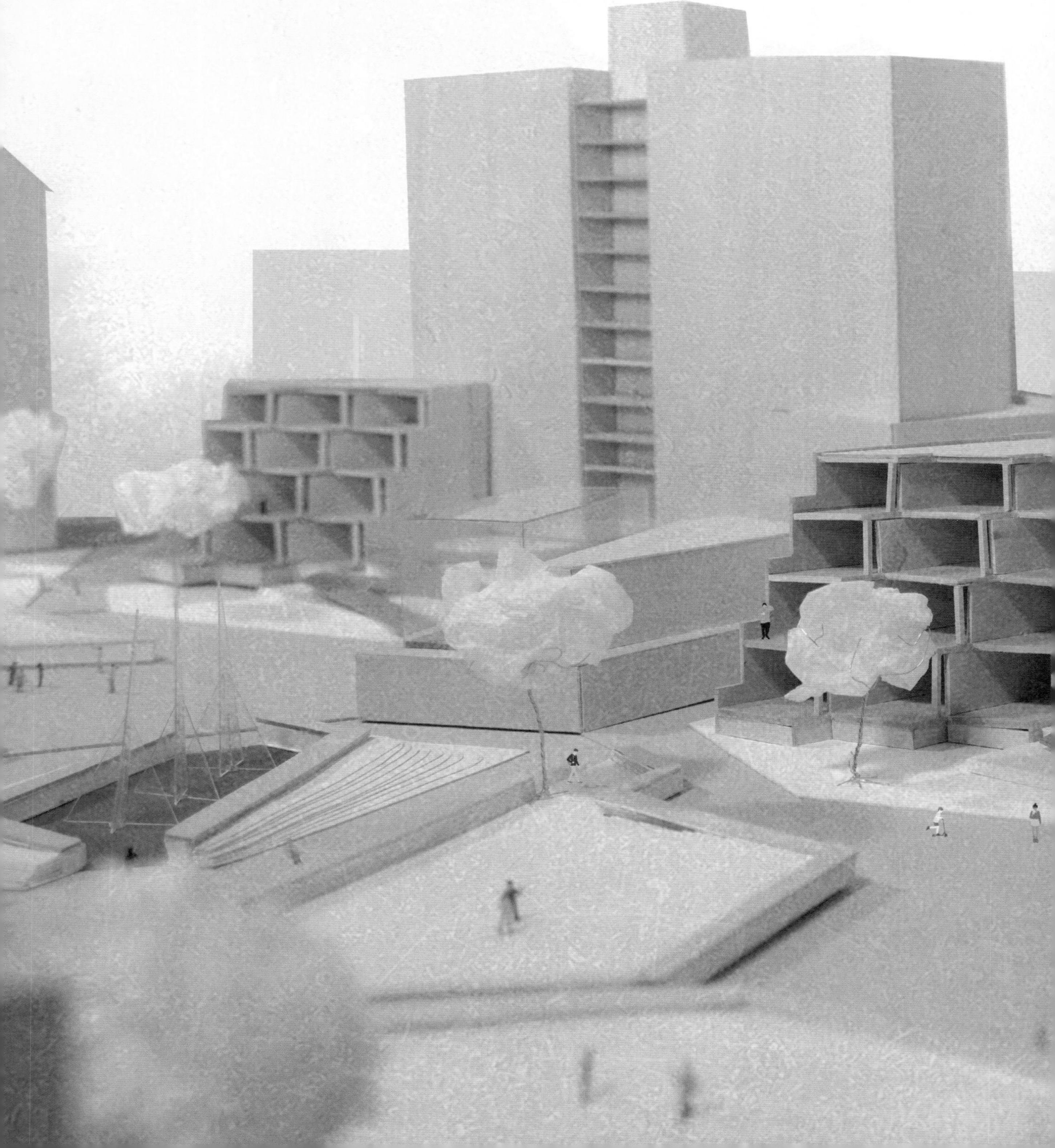

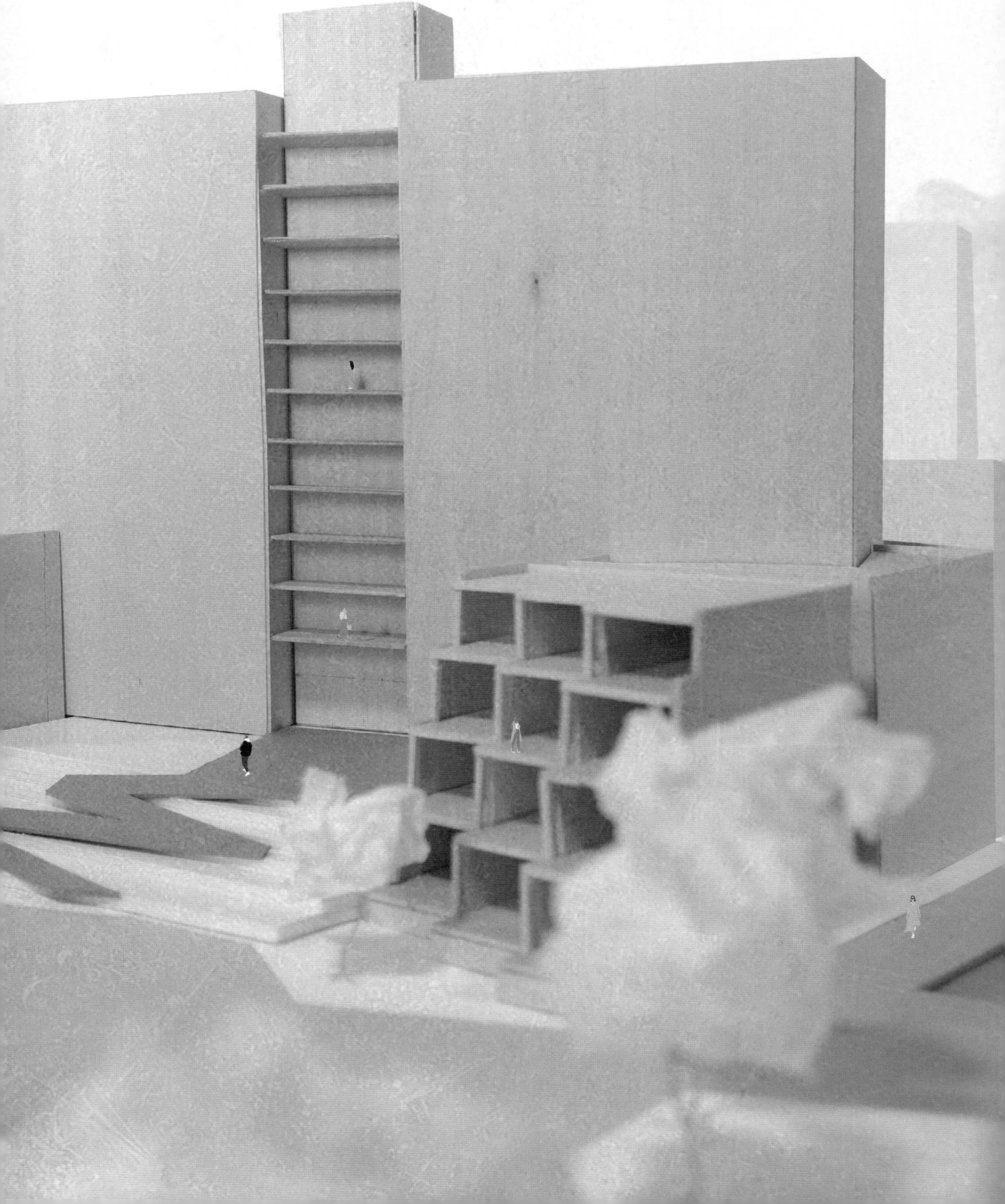

The Interspace: Weaving the Community

Suhyun Jang

Situated between the NYCHA towers and proposed low-rise residential units, this intervention aims to improve the health and wellness of residents through new social spaces with a variety of programs. By interacting, sharing, playing, learning, making, nurturing, and growing in these social spaces, users can develop and maintain a healthy life. Questioning the relationship between form and program, the proposed structures inhabit the leftover space between NYCHA towers and the new residential units to provide a starting point for the community. This space will be transparent, flexible, and permeable, attracting individuals to gather, interact, and form relationships with others while gaining access to natural light and fresh air. The organic curves of the new structures comprise a fluid space that leads guests to the central green space, as well as providing visual access to the exterior for a safer environment. As a way to connect the NYCHA community, the new proposal connects two different scales: the intimate in-between interventions at the ground level to the more public larger scale of the podium. Proposed podium spaces offer collective programs such as a gym and a community space, while interconnected spaces at ground level connect the existing NYCHA residents to new residents of the adjacent low-rise development, increasing chance encounters and social interactions. The new structures provide public shelter and facilitate a sustainable, continuous connection for the community—a place to improve, create, express, relax, and socialize. The spatial interaction catalyzes future change by creating a place within the in-between space.

Ground-Floor Plan

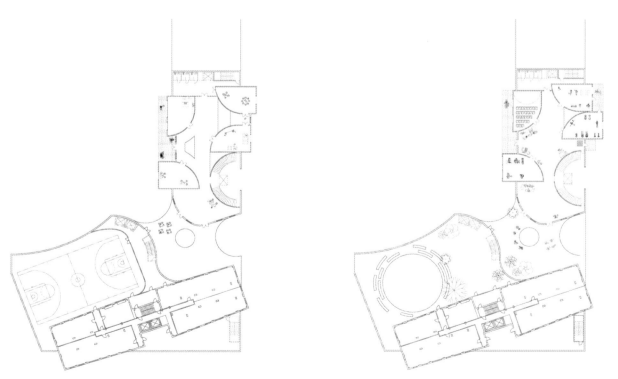

Second-Floor Plan

Third-Floor Plan

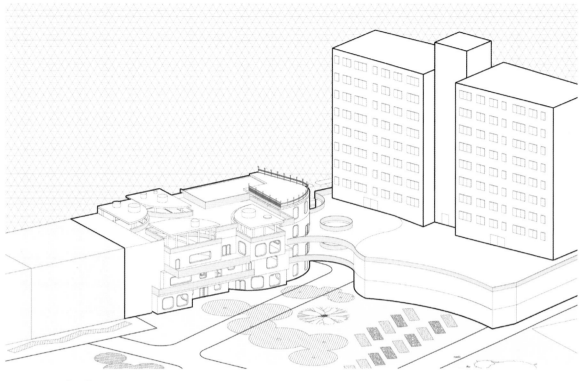

Axonometric View

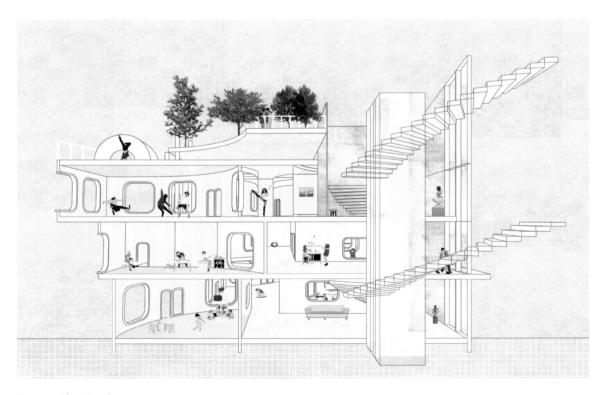

Perspective Section

Rooftop Playground Vignette

Kindergarten

Urban Reciprocity

Dominiq Oti

This proposal offers a model of smaller housing units that aims to cultivate community intimacy and engagement. The apartment blocks function as discrete parts for an intimate scale similar to a large home.

Through the assembly of these discrete parts and carefully programmed spaces, the subset of housing connects to the existing NYCHA tower on the third to fifth floors. Ancillary spaces and services interwoven on the ground and first floors serve the local community. An active departure from the NYCHA towers, the project proposal rethinks current apartment monotony.

Considering the proximity of the public space to the educational facilities, this proposal integrates education as part of the NYCHA block. Individuals of all ages don't need to travel far for educational programs, and after-school programs can support the DREAM Charter School, across the street. The project will contain a small library, a sensory soft play space, and hot-desk office spaces for remote working to promote intergenerational growth, safety, and comfort. As part of the educational program, the project features a public training center that offers a supplementary space for individuals over 21 to gain skills in technology, manual labor, and other expertise for future jobs.

Ground-Floor Plan

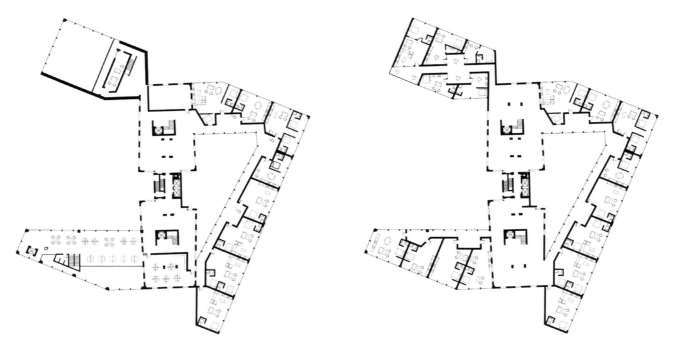

First-Floor Plan

Typical Unit

Diagrammatic Section

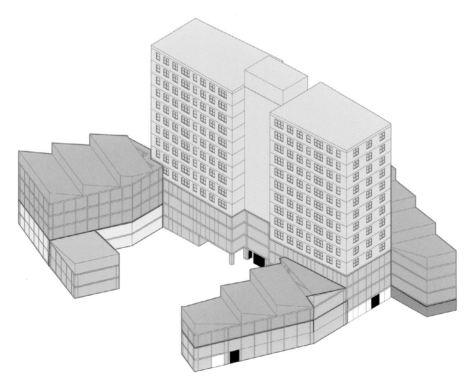

Program Isometric

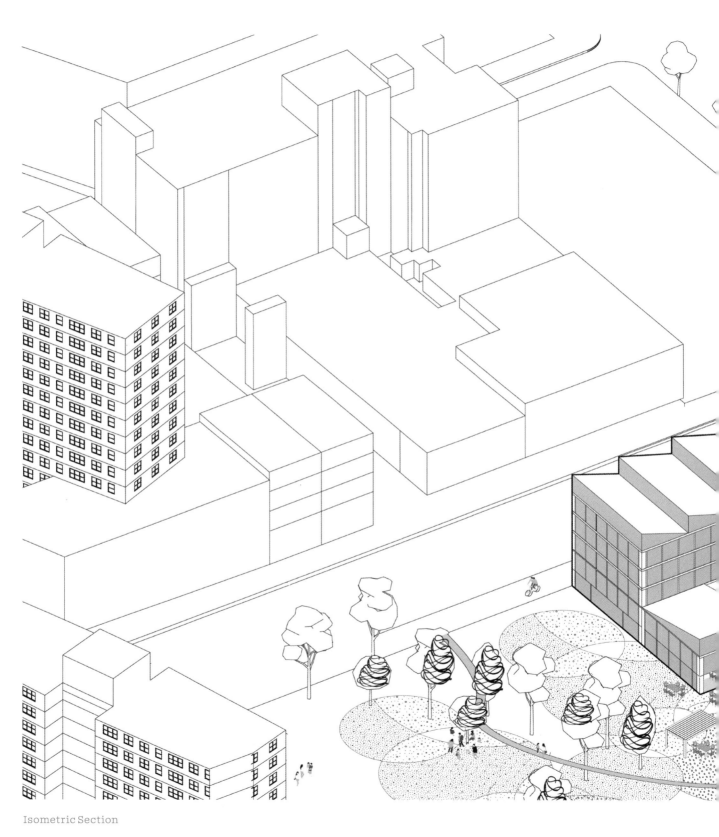

Isometric Section

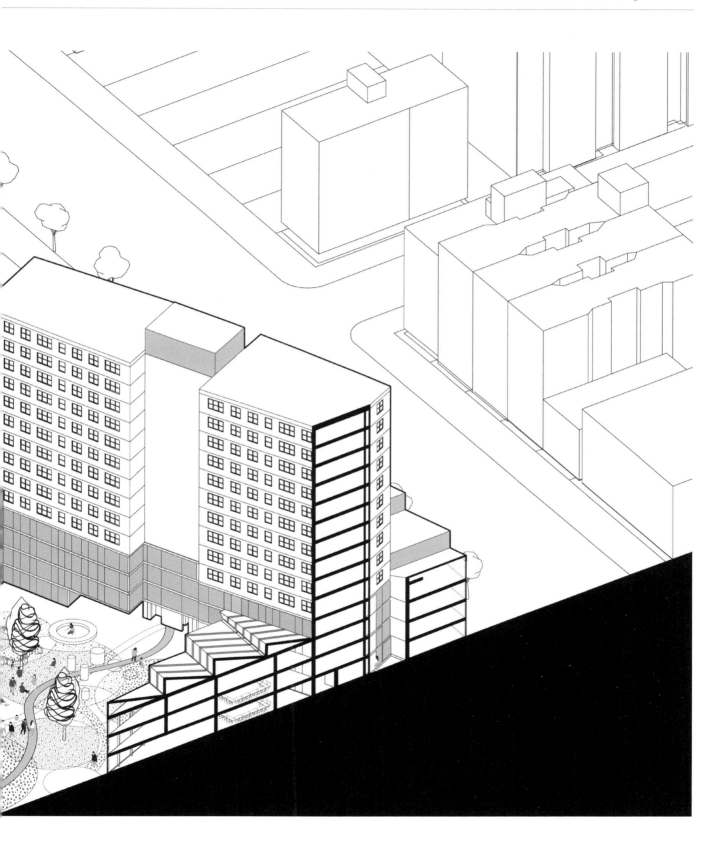

Here Comes the Sun

A Sustainable Future for NYCHA

Raul Martinez Martinez

Developed in 1957, the George Washington Houses quickly became outdated, and the rigid layout of the apartments is unsuitable for the American family. The buildings have barely been refurbished since they were built, and residents are living in poor conditions similar to those NYCHA was trying to eradicate.

This project, "Here Comes the Sun: A Sustainable Future for NYCHA," addresses the most urgent issues facing NYCHA residents today, including unhealthy living conditions, fractured community engagement, and the changing demographics of low-income families. The proposal also builds a flexible and sustainable model that will adapt to future changes in the family. The first stage begins with a full renovation of the interiors, updating amenities like water and heat to current standards. The second stage introduces a new typology for the apartment layouts that is more conducive to contemporary family dynamics. This proposal replaces the isolated rooms connected by a closed hallway with a functional, multipurpose open space that will reinforce interaction between family members. The addition of balconies protected by mobile shutters expands the interior space psychologically, increasing light and ventilation. To facilitate an orientation to natural light, counter monotony, and promote community, each building is characterized by different-colored shutters. The original homogenous layout is replaced by a flexible floor plan with 25 permutations, from studios to four-bedrooms, expanding the plan from eight to twelve apartment units per floor. This changeable organization will allow NYCHA's investment to survive future social and demographic changes.

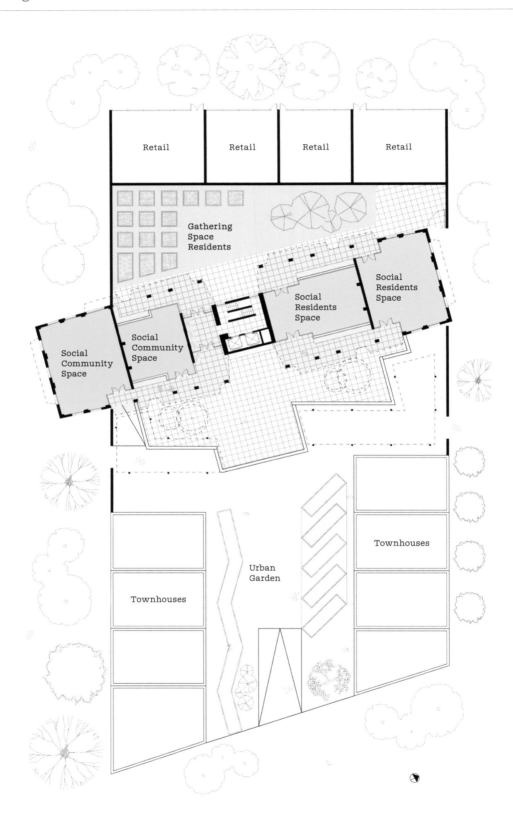

Ground-Floor Plan

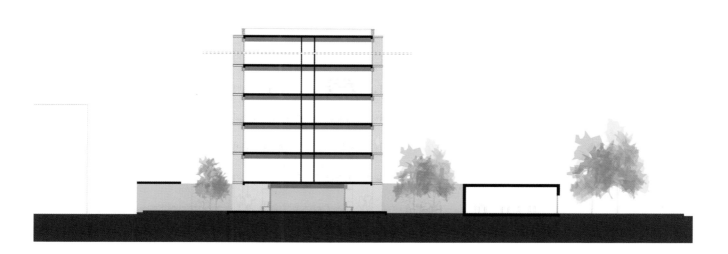

Building Section

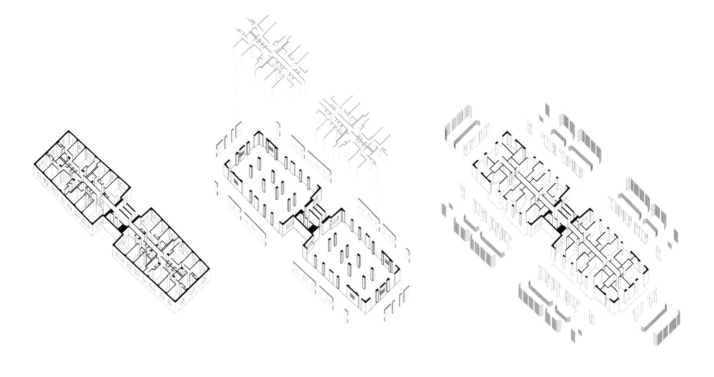

Existing Floor Plan   Proposed Removal and Renovation   Proposed Renovation and Addition

Proposed Renovation and Addition

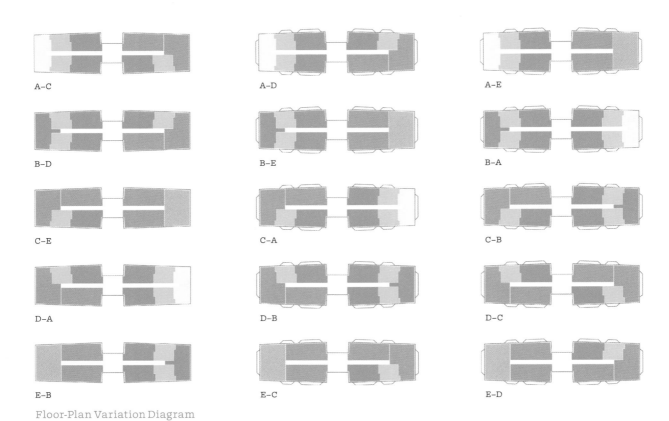

A–C

A–D

A–E

B–D

B–E

B–A

C–E

C–A

C–B

D–A

D–B

D–C

E–B

E–C

E–D

Floor-Plan Variation Diagram

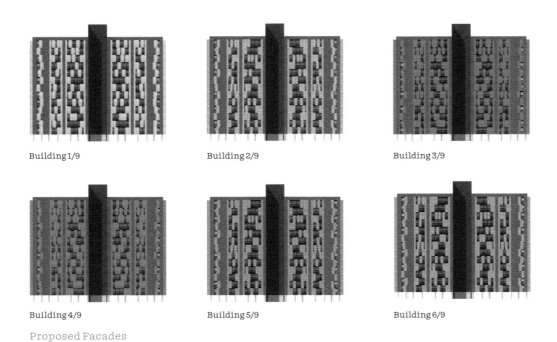

Building 1/9

Building 2/9

Building 3/9

Building 4/9

Building 5/9

Building 6/9

Proposed Facades

Unit Interior View

Exterior View

A Dancing Perimeter Block

David Scurry

This proposal explores the notion of movement within two static perimeter block buildings. Situated in the second southernmost block of the master plan, the project contains two mid-rise residential buildings, each with a large courtyard and a central community pool. The ground floors house extensive community-based programs including a daycare center, a music space, and a gym. The courtyard voids in the building facing the newly proposed avenue are filled in with a public library, a pool in the central void, and a gathering space in the interior of the block. Through a series of formal operations, the ground-floor masonry poché is carved into to create voids of overlap between different uses. Spaces contract and release into large interior rooms, and masonry is eroded to create voids for inviting residential lobbies. The spaces spiral and dance within a normally rigid and fortresslike perimeter block. Brick, concrete, metal, porcelain tile, and wood are improvements over NYCHA's standard materials, especially in the library and gathering space. The upper five floors contain single-loaded residential corridors. The units face out onto the city, and the corridors face onto the courtyards. The facades consist of a series of concrete "string courses" and stepped-back concrete panels, which frame the dancing window units. These staggered upper floors rest on arches of the bottom floor, offering scale to the street front and structural stability to the upper floors.

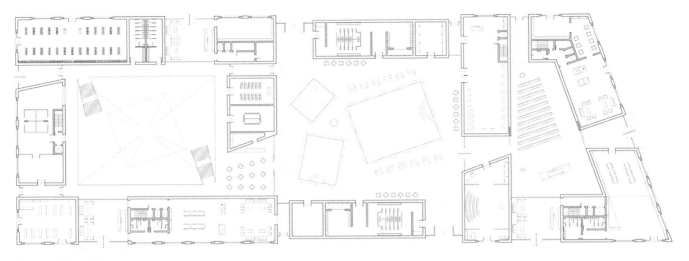

Ground-Floor Plan

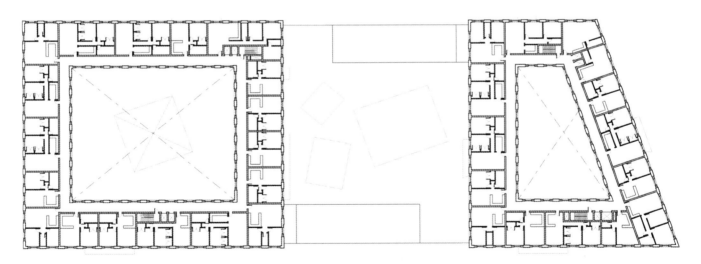

Upper-Floor Plan

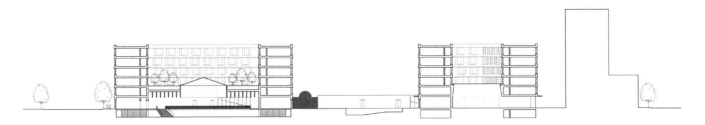

Building Section

Elevation View

Library View

Pool Overlook View

Roof Garden View

Pool Entry

Library View

Brownstone Reimagined

Levi Shaw-Faber

Taking on the low-rise portion of our master plan, this proposal seeks to emphasize the human scale of the iconic brownstone blocks of New York City while updating their functionality for the twenty-first century. Walking down a tree-lined nineteenth-century brownstone block is one of the most pleasurable pedestrian experiences in New York, but those structures—with their narrow rooms, limited natural light, unsuccessful apartment subdivisions, and lack of waste infrastructure—fail to meet today's needs. This proposal features double-wide layouts that include work-from-home spaces, removable kitchens, spiral staircases for easy apartment subdivisions, and highly glazed back walls for increased natural light. The setback glazed penthouses maintain the scale of the four-story brownstone while increasing living space. In addition to the habitable roof space on the street side of the penthouses, all apartments feature balconies providing quiet outdoor space on the garden side. The long balconies also provide privacy for the glazed back wall. Instead of small 20-foot-wide back-yards owned by the residents of each town house, the buildings share a large 250-foot-wide garden, emphasizing a sense of community among the residents.

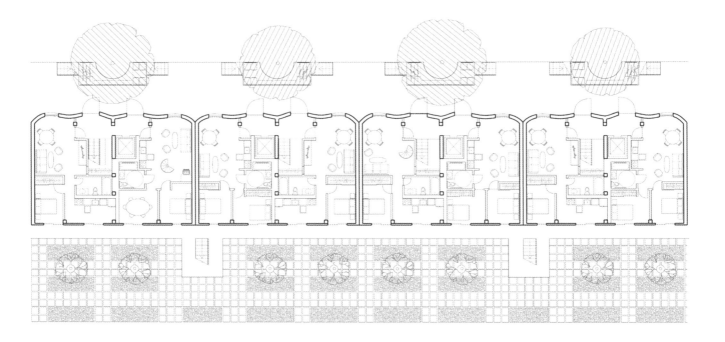

Ground-Floor Plan

View from the Street

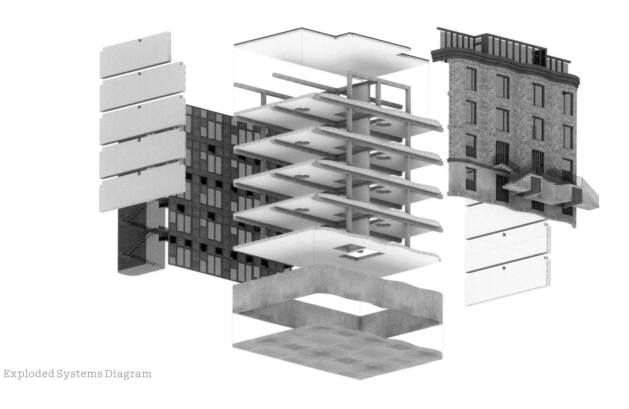

Exploded Systems Diagram

Interior Unit Perspective

Exterior Perspective

Image Credits

Claudia Ansorena
18–19, 30–31, 34, 35

Vignesh Harikrishnan
49

Kohn Pedersen Fox
20, 21, 22, 27, 68–69

Saba Salekfard
8–9, 12–13, 33, 36–37

Nnenna Lynch is the founder of Xylem Projects, a new real estate venture dedicated to preserving housing and creating mixed-use projects throughout the Tri-State area. Lynch has worked in the public sector as senior advisor in economic development to Mayor Bloomberg and as a member of the board of NYCHA. She is a Rhodes Scholar and a five-time track champion in the National Collegiate Athletic Association (NCAA). Lynch is a trustee of Villanova University and a board member of the Association of American Rhodes Scholars, and serves on the New York Road Runners Executive Committee. She graduated Phi Beta Kappa from Villanova University and earned her Master of Letters from Oxford University.

James von Klemperer is president and design principal at Kohn Pedersen Fox Associates, where has worked since 1983. As president of the firm, he is responsible for leading the staff of 750-plus people in ten offices around the world. Von Klemperer has lectured and taught internationally at universities such as Harvard, Columbia, Tsinghua and Tongji, in China, and Seoul National and Yonsei, in Korea, as well as at the European Space Agency, in Paris, and at the conference organized by AMO Rhône-Alpes, in Lyon.

Hana Kassem is a principal at Kohn Pedersen Fox Associates with nearly 30 years of architectural experience. Her human-centric design work focuses on people's experience and perception of the built environment in a variety of typologies and regions. Kassem serves on the AIANY Board of Trustees as VP for Design Excellence and is founding chair of the AIANY Global Dialogue's annual panel "Leaning Out | Women in Architecture." She coedited the book *Architect d.b.a: On Redefining the Roles of the Architect Today.*

Heather Roberge is an architect and educator based in Los Angeles. She is founder and principal of the design practice Murmur and a professor at UCLA Architecture and Urban Design, where she served as chair from 2017 to 2020 and has also directed the undergraduate program. Roberge received the 2017 ACADIA Teaching Award of Excellence and the 2016 Emerging Voices Award from the Architectural League of New York.